The Constitution of the United States

A Look at the Thirteenth and Fourteenth Amendments

Slavery Abolished, Equal Protection Established

JOHN RICHARD CONWAY, ESQ.

MyReportLinks.com Books

an imprint of

Enslow Publishers, Inc.

Box 398, 40 Industrial Road
Berkeley Heights, NJ 07922
USA

MyReportLinks.com Books, an imprint of Enslow Publishers, Inc. MyReportLinks®
is a registered trademark of Enslow Publishers, Inc.

Library of Congress Cataloging-in-Publication Data

Conway, John Richard, 1969–
  A look at the Thirteenth and Fourteenth Amendments : slavery abolished, equal
protection established / John Richard Conway.
     p. cm. — (Constitution of the United States)
  Includes bibliographical references and index.
  ISBN-13: 978-1-59845-070-5 (hardcover)
  ISBN-10: 1-59845-070-0 (hardcover)
   1. Slavery—Law and legislation—United States—History. 2. Equality before the law—
United States—History. 3. United States. Constitution. 13th Amendment. 4. United
States. Constitution. 14th Amendment. 5. Slaves—Legal status, laws, etc.—United States—
History. 6. African Americans—Civil rights—History—19th century. 7. Slavery—United
States—History. I. Title.
KF4545.S5C66 2008
342.7308'7—dc22

                                    2007019729

Printed in the United States of America

10 9 8 7 6 5 4 3 2 1

To Our Readers:
Through the purchase of this book, you and your library gain access to the Report Links that specifically back
up this book.
The Publisher will provide access to the Report Links that back up this book and will keep these Report Links
up to date on **www.myreportlinks.com** for five years from the book's first publication date.
We have done our best to make sure all Internet addresses in this book were active and appropriate when we
went to press. However, the author and the Publisher have no control over, and assume no liability for, the
material available on those Internet sites or on other Web sites they may link to.
The usage of the MyReportLinks.com Books Web site is subject to the terms and conditions stated on the Usage
Policy Statement on **www.myreportlinks.com**.
A password may be required to access the Report Links that back up this book. The password is found on the
bottom of page 4 of this book.
Any comments or suggestions can be sent by e-mail to comments@myreportlinks.com or to the address on the
back cover.

✿ Enslow Publishers, Inc. is committed to printing our books on recycled paper. The paper in every book
contains between 10% to 30% post-consumer waste (PCW). The cover board on the outside of each book contains 100% PCW. Our goal is to do our part to help young people and the environment too!

Photo Credits: Americancivilwar.com, p. 41; AP/Wide World Photos, p. 104; Ashbrook Center for Public
Affairs, p. 62; BlackPast.org, p. 77; CBCNews.com, p. 101; Constitutional Rights Foundation, p. 85;
CORBIS/Bettmann, p. 93 (Lovings); Cornell University, pp. 30, 103; Enslow Publishers, Inc., p. 35; FindLaw, a
Thomson Reuters business, pp. 53, 64; Florida State Archives: Woody Wisner, p. 89; History Matters, p. 66;
Justia, p. 107; Library of Congress, pp. 8, 10, 12, 20, 21, 28, 31, 32, 33, 37, 40, 43, 46–47, 50, 70–71, 74, 78,
86–87, 96; Long Island University, p. 38; MyReportLinks.com Books, p. 4; National Archives, p. 27; National
Park Service, p. 48; PBS, pp. 19, 26, 59; Shutterstock.com, pp. 16–17, 54, 81, 92–93; The University of
Minnesota, p. 61; The University of Missouri-Kansas City School of Law, p. 49; The University of North
Carolina, p. 22; U.S. Department of State, pp. 99, 102; U.S. Courts, p. 58; U.S. Supreme Court, pp. 100, 106;
Washington University, p. 36; The White House, p. 11; Yale University, p. 25.

Cover Photo: Library of Congress

CONTENTS

MyReportLinks.com Books
Great Books, Great Links, Great for Research!

The Internet sites featured in this book can save you hours of research time. These Internet sites—we call them *"Report Links"*—are constantly changing, but we keep them up to date on our Web site.

When you see this "Approved Web Site" logo, you will know that we are directing you to a great Internet site that will help you with your research.

Give it a try! Type http://www.myreportlinks.com into your browser, click on the series title and enter the password, then click on the book title, and scroll down to the Report Links listed for this book.

The Report Links will bring you to great source documents, photographs, and illustrations. MyReportLinks.com Books save you time, feature Report Links that are kept up to date, and make report writing easier than ever! A complete listing of the Report Links can be found on pages 118–119 at the back of the book.

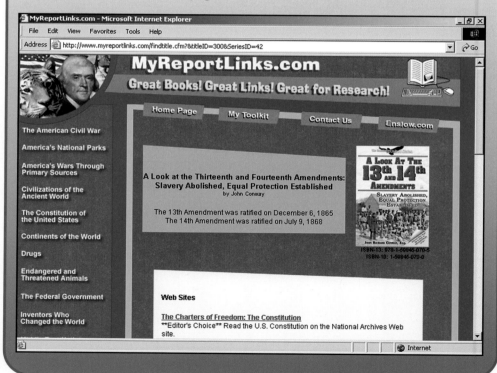

Please see "To Our Readers" on the copyright page for important information about this book, the MyReportLinks.com Web site, and the Report Links that back up this book.

Please enter TFA1787 if asked for a password.

TIME LINE

1619 —Dutch traders introduce first African slaves to the Virginia colony at Jamestown.

1654 —John Casor becomes the first person to be legally recognized as a slave in America.

1776 —*July 4:* Declaration of Independence is issued. Sections denouncing slavery have been deleted.

1787 —*May 25:* The Philadelphia Convention meets to revise the Articles of Confederation and instead drafts a new constitution.

1789 —Ratified by the necessary states in 1788, the new government of the United States begins operating under the Constitution on March 4.

1793 —The Fugitive Slave Act of 1793 is passed.

1850 —Fugitive Slave law of 1850 is passed by Congress, angering many abolitionists in the North.

1857 —The United States Supreme Court hears *Dred Scott v. Sanford,* affirming the principle that slaves are indeed property.

1861 —*April 12:* Shots are fired at Fort Sumter in Charleston, South Carolina, beginning the American Civil War.

1862 —*September 22:* The Emancipation Proclamation is issued after the Battle of Antietam.

1865 —*January 31:* the Thirteenth Amendment abolishing slavery is proposed in Congress.

—*April 9:* General Robert E. Lee surrenders his army at Appomattox Court House, effectively ending the American Civil War.

—*December 6:* The Thirteenth Amendment is ratified and goes into effect.

1866 —*June 16:* The Fourteenth Amendment granting citizenship and extending due process and equal protection to all native-born people is proposed to Congress.

1868 —*July 28:* The Fourteenth Amendment is ratified and goes into effect.

1873 —The U.S. Supreme Court hears the *Slaughter-House Cases,* the first major challenge to the Fourteenth Amendment.

1883 —The *Civil Rights Cases* are decided. The Supreme Court holds that the Fourteenth Amendment applies only to governmental, and not private, action.

1896 —In *Plessy* v. *Ferguson,* the Supreme Court rules that racial segregation is acceptable introducing the doctrine of "separate by equal facilities."

1925 —In *Gitlow* v. *New York,* the Supreme Court determines that the Fourteenth Amendment applies the Bill of Rights to all state and local governmental action, not just federal governmental actions.

1954 —*Brown* v. *Board of Education* is decided, undercutting *Plessy* v. *Ferguson's* "separate but equal" doctrine as it applied to the schools.

1995 —Mississippi unofficially ratifies the Thirteenth Amendment.

LIFE DURING WARTIME 1

O n September 17, 1862, more than 23,000 men were killed or wounded at Sharpsburg, Maryland, during the Battle of Antietam. It was—and remains—the single bloodiest day in American history.

The American Civil War, or the War Between the States, had been raging since April 1861. Now, more than a year later, the South and its Army of Northern Virginia, led by General Robert E. Lee, had been defeated and pushed back into Virginia by the North's Army of the Potomac, led by General George B. McClellan.

The victory was significant because it was the first major battle of the Civil War fought on northern soil, and it was the first major battle in the critical Eastern Theater won by union forces in almost two years of fighting. The Eastern Theater included Virginia, West Virginia, Maryland, Pennsylvania, the coastal areas of North Carolina, and Washington, D.C. Most of the major battles of the war took place in the Eastern

▲ After the Union Army's victory in the Battle of Antietam on September 17, 1862, President Abraham Lincoln issued the Emancipation Proclamation freeing slaves. Lincoln (center) stands with Allan Pinkerton (left), and Maj. Gen. John A. McClernand (right) at Antietam.

Theater. In addition, this area was important because it included many of the country's most populated cities, was near the capitals of both the United States (Washington, D.C.) and the Confederate States (Richmond, Virginia), and was home to some of the country's largest and most important newspapers.

The victory at Antietam was critical because it gave President Abraham Lincoln the power to issue the Emancipation Proclamation freeing slaves. Lincoln's bold decision fundamentally altered the character of the Civil War, changing it from a war to hold the United States together into a moral crusade to abolish the institution of slavery.[1]

Lincoln had considered the possibility of issuing a proclamation that would end slavery as early as July 1862. However, he decided against making an official statement because he did not want to appear desperate; that is, he did not want people to think that he was desperately trying to rally northern support in a losing cause. Until Antietam, the Union forces had been consistently beaten by the Confederate forces—and if the South won, slavery would remain legal. Lincoln needed his Union Army to win a major battle, so that he could be seen as issuing the Proclamation from a position of strength and not weakness.[1]

Issuing the Emancipation Proclamation was risky—some people feared it would upset a group

Issued on September 22, 1862, the Emancipation Proclamation went into effect on January 1, 1863. This important document did not free all the slaves in the United States. Instead, it freed those in rebellious southern states. However, it was a critical step on the road to the abolition of slavery.

of Northern democrats called "copperheads," people who did not support Lincoln's effort to keep the Union together by going to war. There was also a sense that several border states—states that had legalized slavery but had not seceded from the Union—might change course and support the Confederacy.

In addition, Lincoln's legal basis for issuing such a proclamation was somewhat shaky. As a peacetime president, Lincoln had no authority to free any slaves anywhere. However, Lincoln felt that in times of war, and as commander in chief of the United States military, he had the authority to issue a proclamation to free the slaves in certain

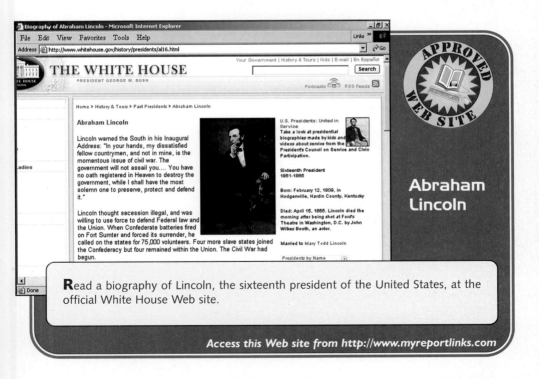

Read a biography of Lincoln, the sixteenth president of the United States, at the official White House Web site.

Access this Web site from http://www.myreportlinks.com

Shot by John Wilkes Booth on April 14, 1865, Lincoln led the United States through one of its darkest times, the Civil War. By fighting to preserve the union and to end slavery, Lincoln built the foundation of a better and stronger union.

territories. Thus the Emancipation Proclamation was a military order issued by Lincoln in his capacity as commander in chief. It was not a statute enacted by Congress, or a constitutional amendment.

The Emancipation Proclamation allowed slaves to enlist in the United States military—and nearly two hundred thousand African Americans did. Most were ex-slaves. This gave the North a critical supply of additional manpower that the South would not have until the very closing days of the war.[2]

A draft of the proclamation was issued on September 22, 1862; the final draft took effect on January 1, 1863. It said that all slaves would be permanently freed from slavery in all Confederate territories that had not returned to the United States by January 1, 1863. The Proclamation intentionally excluded the Union slave states of Maryland, Delaware, Missouri, and Kentucky. There were also many specific exemptions for counties of Confederate states already in Union control at the time, as well as the counties that made up the new state of West Virginia, which had recently seceded from the state of Virginia, which had itself seceded from the United States.[3]

The Emancipation Proclamation did not free all of the slaves in the United States. It did not even free slaves in former Confederate territory that was now held by the Union forces. In theory, it only freed those slaves held in rebel states, and it was only implemented as Union forces pushed into Confederate territory. However, it was a critical step in the abolition of slavery in the United States, and it set the stage for the permanent abolition of slavery by the Thirteenth Amendment to the United States Constitution.

THE HISTORY OF SLAVERY

2

Human slavery is an ancient institution, dating back to the dawn of history. It was practiced in most ancient cultures including those of Egypt, Mesopotamia, Greece, Rome, Persia, China, Africa, and Medieval Europe.

In the sixteenth and seventeenth centuries, Europeans and Africans began what became known as the Atlantic slave trade. Europeans bought slaves in West Africa and transported them to their colonies in the Caribbean, South America, and to the country that became the United States. Europeans believed that Africans were accustomed to working in hot, tropical climates and were immune to tropical diseases that made working in these areas dangerous for Europeans. Of course, they did not consider that these same African slaves were not immune to European diseases. As a result, when these Africans came into contact with their new masters, their populations were ravaged by diseases such as smallpox.

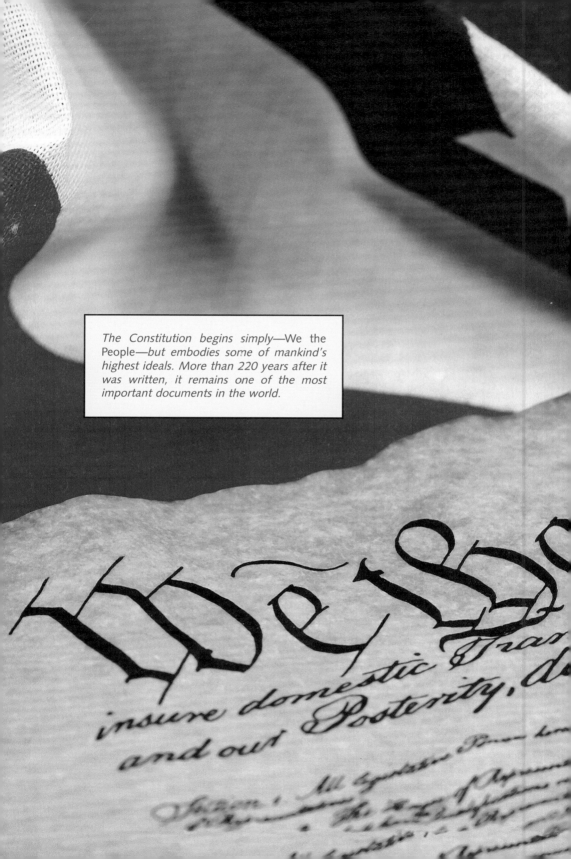

The Constitution begins simply—We the People—but embodies some of mankind's highest ideals. More than 220 years after it was written, it remains one of the most important documents in the world.

eople

uility, provide for the commo
rdain and establish this Con

...be vested in a Congress of the United States, which shall co...

...l be composed of Members chosen every second Year by the People
...of the several Branch of the State Legislature.
...all not have attained to the Age of twenty five Years, and been...
...of that State in which he shall be chosen.
...of Persons, including those bound to Se...
...which may be included with...
...shall be made within three Years after...
...by Law direct. The Numbe...

In 1619, Dutch traders introduced African slaves to the Virginia Colony at Jamestown, a farming community that was in search of cheap labor to tend to its crops. The English who lived in the colony worked in "peonage," a system that forced individuals to repay a debt through labor, in this case, the cost of transportation to the New World. This was also called indentured servitude. In general, the colonist (and sometimes his family as well) would agree to work for a patron (the person who paid their travel costs) for a term that generally could not exceed seven years. The written contract was known as an "indenture," hence the term, "indentured servant."[1]

DRAWBACKS OF INDENTURED SERVITUDE

Indentured servants provided labor, but there were costs to the person who held the indenture. Once an indentured servant's term was up, they were free to go about their business, and their patron was left to find new workers. This was an expensive process. Even worse from a business standpoint, the patron had to keep an eye on his indentured servants to make sure they did not try to break their contract.

But worse of all, as far as the patrons were concerned, there were limits to what a patron could do to control their workforce, because indentured servants still had rights under English common law. Slavery would provide a more economically feasible and simple alternative—slaves were property, a commodity that could be bought and sold and punished without consequences. And when a slave died, he or she only had to be replaced. And because they were property, slaves had virtually no rights, so enforcing a master's will was much easier than enforcing a patron's contract.

Initially, the first African slaves brought to America were treated as indentured servants. That changed when John Casor filed suit against Anthony Johnson in 1654.

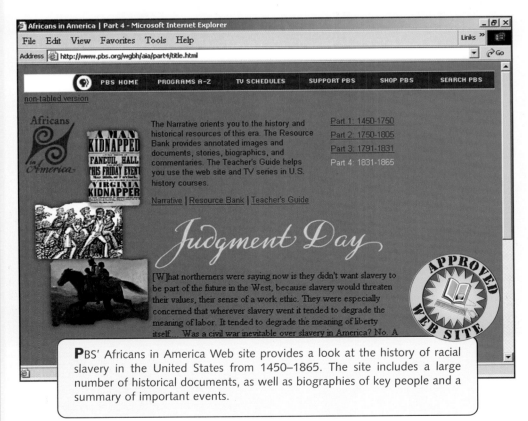

PBS' Africans in America Web site provides a look at the history of racial slavery in the United States from 1450–1865. The site includes a large number of historical documents, as well as biographies of key people and a summary of important events.

▲ Thomas Jefferson is widely admired as one of this country's greatest citizens. The third President of the United States and one of the primary authors of the Declaration of Independence, Jefferson included a denunciation of slavery in one of the early drafts of the Declaration. Yet Jefferson himself was a slave owner.

THE FIRST SLAVE

Anthony Johnson, a black man, was one of the first indentured servants brought to Virginia by the Dutch in 1619. He earned his freedom and became a wealthy landowner in the colony with indentured servants of his own. One of them, John Casor, an African, claimed that he came to the Virginia colony as an indentured servant, and therefore had the right to transfer his service to someone other than Johnson. Johnson filed suit

▽ *The Founding Fathers wrote the Declaration of Independence in order to express their desire to be free of the King and control their own destiny. Sadly, the Founding Fathers were divided on the question of freedom for African Americans.*

against the other master, Robert Parker, arguing that Casor was Johnson's servant for life. The Virginia Colony court upheld Johnson's claim.[2] It is the first record of a person being declared a slave in this country.

Because the cash crops of the southern colonies of British North America were tobacco, cotton, and indigo—labor-intensive crops that required significant man-hours to plant, grow, and harvest—slavery was essential to the colonies'

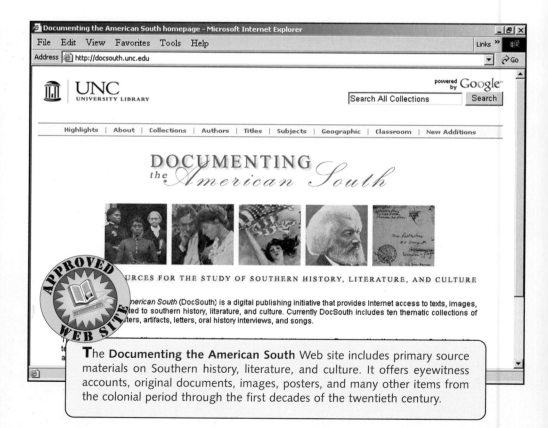

The Documenting the American South Web site includes primary source materials on Southern history, literature, and culture. It offers eyewitness accounts, original documents, images, posters, and many other items from the colonial period through the first decades of the twentieth century.

economic success. Initially, each of what would become the original thirteen states were British colonies that allowed slavery in the seventeenth century. However, the institution of slavery was most common in Maryland, Virginia, North and South Carolina and Georgia.

On the eve of the American Revolution, slavery was a sore subject. Many people thought it was hypocritical for men to argue for their own freedom (from the British king), yet at the same time keep other men in bondage. Thomas Jefferson included a denunciation of the practice of slavery in the original draft of the Declaration of Independence, accusing the British king of: "wag[ing] cruel war against human nature itself, violating its most sacred rights of life and liberty in the persons of a distant people who never offended him, captivating and carrying them into slavery in another hemisphere, or to incur miserable death in their transportation thither."[3]

This line angered southern representatives, and it was removed from the final draft of the Declaration.

➡ANY PORT IN A STORM

During the American Revolution, about five thousand slaves fought for the Americans. George Washington, desperate for manpower, lifted the ban on slave enlistment (the U.S. Army would not be integrated again until President Harry Truman integrated the armed services on July 26, 1948. Nearly one hundred years after the Emancipation Proclamation, President Truman's decision was still wildly controversial). The British offered freedom to any slave who would fight for the King. While few slaves fought against the Americans, thousands of former slaves worked as paid laborers for the British forces. Perhaps as many as one hundred thousand escaped to British lines and freedom.[4]

After the Revolution, the newly—independent states continued to work together under the Articles of Confederation, which functioned as a military alliance between the separate states. It wasn't long before the newly-independent states realized that running a country was a complicated business. In other words, the original thirteen states came to understand that the Articles did not do enough to regulate the new union. In an effort to refine the Articles and make them stronger, delegates from each colony met in Philadelphia in the spring of 1787.

⊜SLAVERY AND THE CONSTITUTION

The original goal of the Constitutional Convention, as it came to be known, was just to make some changes to the Articles of Confederation, not redo them. But a few delegates had a different idea and instead the Convention moved toward the development of a completely new framework of government.

By September, the convention, led by George Washington, had created a government with a legislative branch (represented by Congress), a chief executive (the president), and an independent judiciary. This government, designed largely by James Madison, was very controversial.

Men who supported the new constitution were called "Federalists" and were led by Alexander Hamilton and John Jay of New York and James Madison of Virginia. These men lobbied their state legislatures for passage of the new constitution.

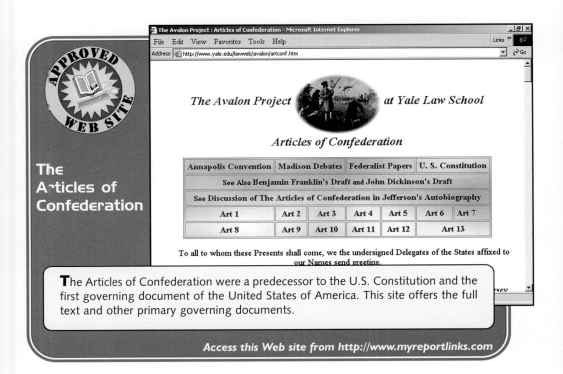

The Articles of Confederation

The Avalon Project : Articles of Confederation - Microsoft Internet Explorer

File   Edit   View   Favorites   Tools   Help

Address http://www.yale.edu/lawweb/avalon/artconf.htm

The Avalon Project   *at Yale Law School*

Articles of Confederation

Annapolis Convention	Madison Debates	Federalist Papers		U. S. Constitution
See Also Benjamin Franklin's Draft and John Dickinson's Draft				
See Discussion of The Articles of Confederation in Jefferson's Autobiography				
Art 1	Art 2	Art 3	Art 4	Art 5	Art 6	Art 7
Art 8	Art 9	Art 10	Art 11	Art 12	Art 13	

To all to whom these Presents shall come, we the undersigned Delegates of the States affixed to our Names send greeting.

The Articles of Confederation were a predecessor to the U.S. Constitution and the first governing document of the United States of America. This site offers the full text and other primary governing documents.

Access this Web site from http://www.myreportlinks.com

Their powerful series of essays supporting the new constitution, known as *The Federalist Papers,* were originally printed in New York newspapers before being reprinted in newspapers throughout the thirteen states.[5]

An equally prominent group of this country's founders was strongly opposed to the new Constitution. These men, known as Anti-Federalists, were concerned that the document gave too much power to a central government; to them, a strong, centralized government looked too much like a

The **Slavery and the Making of America** Web site includes a wealth of information on American slavery. Photographs, tape-recorded firsthand accounts of life under slavery and Reconstruction, journals, and diaries help paint a picture of what it was like to be a slave.

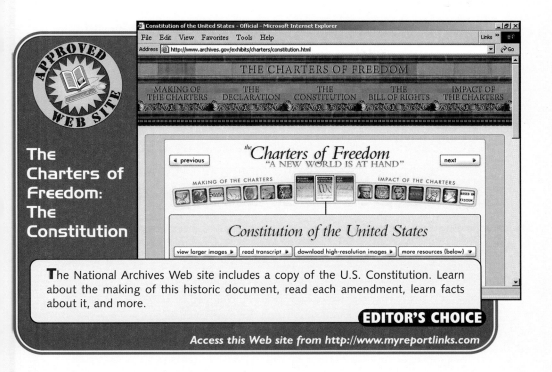

The
Charters of
Freedom:
The
Constitution

THE CHARTERS OF FREEDOM

MAKING OF
THE CHARTERS
THE
DECLARATION
THE
CONSTITUTION
THE
BILL OF RIGHTS
IMPACT OF
THE CHARTERS

the *Charters of Freedom*
"A NEW WORLD IS AT HAND"

◀ previous
next ▶

MAKING OF THE CHARTERS
IMPACT OF THE CHARTERS

Constitution of the United States

view larger images ▶   read transcript ▶   download high-resolution images ▶   more resources (below) ▼

The National Archives Web site includes a copy of the U.S. Constitution. Learn about the making of this historic document, read each amendment, learn facts about it, and more.

EDITOR'S CHOICE

Access this Web site from http://www.myreportlinks.com

monarchy, a type of government these men had just fought to overturn.

Disagreements aside, slavery once again proved to be a thorny issue. In the proposed new government, legislative representation would be decided by state population—the greater the population, the more seats in the legislature. Furthermore, the amount of money each state contributed to the new government would be based on population. Roughly twenty percent of the population of the new United States was made up of slaves. As much as half of the population of several southern states was slaves.

Southerners wanted slaves to count as people so they would have greater representation in the new government, but they also wanted slaves to count as property so they would not have to pay so much in taxes. In that way, the South could benefit from increased participation in government, as slaves could not vote, yet its citizens would not be liable for additional taxes. Northern

▲ In 1793, Eli Whitney invented the cotton gin (shown here), a machine that made it much easier to process cotton. Whitney's invention transformed cotton into the South's most important crop and led directly to the South's increased dependence on slave labor.

states tended to take the opposite view, believing slaves should be taxed as property but not be counted towards representation. The two sides compromised, determining that each slave would count as three-fifths of a citizen for both representation and taxation. In other words, as far as representation was concerned, five slaves would equal three free people.

Debates about slavery continued in the new union. Georgia, North Carolina, and South Carolina threatened to withdraw if slavery was made illegal. The other ten states had already banned the importation of new slaves. Because of the threat from the three slave states, Congress decided to delay any ban on the importation of slaves for twenty years. With these compromises in place, the new constitution was ratified. But the seeds of future controversy had been planted.[6]

⊖ The Cotton Gin

By the late eighteenth century, it was generally believed that slavery would be phased out over time. Most Northern states had made the practice illegal. However, in 1793, Eli Whitney invented the cotton gin. This machine sped up cotton processing and transformed cotton into the leading cash crop for most new Southern states. As a result, the demand for cotton increased and the institution of slavery in cotton-growing states was reenergized.

Regardless, in 1808, twenty years after the passage of the Constitution, the United States government did finally ban the importation of slaves.[7]

In the northern United States, a number of groups favored the abolition—or outlawing—of slavery. They came to be known as "abolitionists." They began to push for an end to slavery. In the 1820s an abolitionist group called the American Colonization Society developed the idea that freeing slaves was not the best solution. However, though these abolitionists wanted to free slaves, they did not want them to be living among them

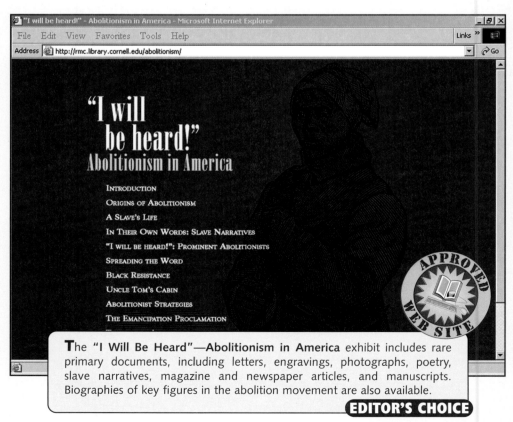

The "I Will Be Heard"—Abolitionism in America exhibit includes rare primary documents, including letters, engravings, photographs, poetry, slave narratives, magazine and newspaper articles, and manuscripts. Biographies of key figures in the abolition movement are also available.

EDITOR'S CHOICE

UNITED STATES SLAVE TRADE.
1850.

▲ *While the abolition movement became more popular in the North in the early nineteenth century, the slave trade continued to flourish. This engraving depicts slaves, including a mother and her children (right), being sold to a trader on horseback.*

in society. Instead, they decided it would be best to return slaves to Africa. And in 1821, they established the colony of Liberia, which is on the west coast of Africa. Over the next forty-or-so years, thousands of former slaves were shipped to the colony which became an independent state in 1847. But by the 1850s, enthusiasm for the project had disappeared. Abolitionists would need to find another solution. (Many of today's Liberian citizens are descendants of the slaves brought to the country almost two hundred years ago).

The *Fugitive Slave Act* passed in 1850 made it legal for groups of men, or posses, to track down slaves that had escaped from their owners. The drawing above shows four slaves, two of them apparently wounded, being ambushed by six armed men.

Meanwhile, tensions were growing between Northern free states and Southern slave states. In 1793, the federal government passed a fugitive slave law, which made it a federal crime to help a slave escape. The law, an attempt to settle disputes between free and slave states, made it possible to recapture escaped slaves who had managed to escape to a free state.

However, free states worked around the law, or at least were good at delaying its implementation. Because some states did not want to return a free African American into slavery, many required a trial before an escaped slave could be returned to a slave state. Northern juries refused to convict people accused of violating the 1793 law. Most damaging was the Supreme Court's 1842 decision in *Prigg v. Pennsylvania,* which led several northern states to pass laws that made it made it illegal for any state official to interfere with runaway slaves or otherwise help with their recapture. The Fugitive Slave Act of 1793 was still the law, but it was much weaker than the government had intended it to be.

Abolition, Anti-Slavery Movements, and the Rise of Sectional Controversy

APPROVED WEB SITE

African American Odyssey: Abolition, Anti-Slavery Movements, and the Rise of the Sectional Cont - Microsoft Internet Explorer

File   Edit   View   Favorites   Tools   Help   Links

Address http://memory.loc.gov/ammem/aaohtml/exhibit/aopart3b.html

Abolition, Anti-Slavery Movements, and the Rise of the Sectional Controversy

Part 1

Part 2: Fugitive Slave Law | Growing Sectionalism | Militant Abolition | "The Book That Made This Great War"

Fugitive Slave Law

North to Canada

REPORT FOR THE YEAR 1858—9.

The Fugitive Slave Law passed in 1850 required government employees to arrest runaway slaves or risk being fined $1,000. Read the law on this site. You can also view other primary documents and historical images relating to the African-American experience.

Access this Web site from http://www.myreportlinks.com

States in the South responded by getting Congress to enact the Fugitive Slave Law of 1850, which stated that any federal or state official who did not arrest an alleged runaway slave would be liable to a fine of one thousand dollars. Law-enforcement officials everywhere were now bound by law to arrest anyone suspected of being a runaway slave.

And very little evidence was needed to justify an arrest—a sworn testimony of ownership was enough. Under the 1850 act, the suspected slave could not even ask for a jury trial or testify on his or her own behalf. The end result was that even a free African American could be made a slave on just the sworn testimony of an "owner." Also, the Fugitive Slave Law stated that anyone providing food or shelter to a runaway slave was subject to six months in prison and a one-thousand-dollar fine. Thus anyone who assisted a runaway slave could be liable for severe criminal penalties.[8]

→LAWS TO COMBAT THE FUGITIVE SLAVE LAW

The new law put moderate abolitionists in a bind—either they disobey the law at the risk of severe punishment, or they abandon their principles. Many northerners felt their government had been hijacked to support slavery, a practice they hated. In an attempt to weaken the 1850 Fugitive Slave Law, many states passed Personal Liberty

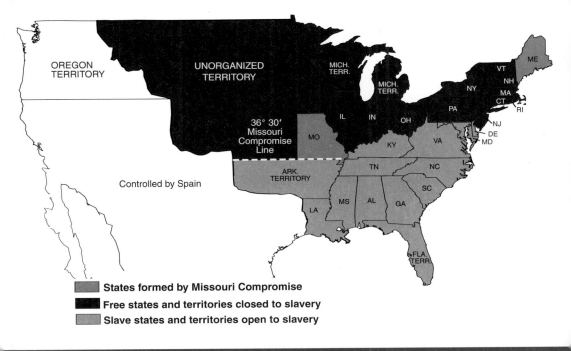

OREGON TERRITORY

UNORGANIZED TERRITORY

MICH. TERR.

MICH. TERR.

VT

ME

NH

NY

MA

CT

PA

RI

NJ

DE

MD

IL

IN

OH

36° 30′ Missouri Compromise Line

MO

KY

VA

Controlled by Spain

ARK. TERRITORY

TN

NC

SC

MS

AL

GA

LA

FLA. TERR.

States formed by Missouri Compromise

Free states and territories closed to slavery

Slave states and territories open to slavery

▲ *Disagreements over slavery intensified as America expanded to the west in the nineteenth century. The Missouri Compromise of 1850 was intended to appease both sides: Slavery would be regulated in the new Western territories and prohibited in the former Louisiana Territory north of 36° 30′ latitude except within the boundaries of the proposed state of Missouri.*

Laws, which prevented state officials from enforcing the 1850 slave act.

Meanwhile, as America expanded to the west, disagreements about slavery intensified. Many northerners felt any new states and territories should be slave-free. But many southerners wanted to balance free and slave states to protect the institution of slavery.

In 1820, abolitionists and the pro-slavery groups in the U.S. Congress devised the Missouri Compromise, an agreement which regulated slavery in the Western territories and prohibited slavery in the former Louisiana Territory north of 36° 30′ latitude, except within the boundaries of the proposed state of Missouri. In newly settled territories such as Kansas, violence flared up between free and slave settlers.[9]

⊖ DRED SCOTT AND ITS AFTERMATH

In 1857, the United States Supreme Court tried to calm the fears of the pro-slavery faction when it heard the *Dred Scott* v. *Sanford* case. But instead

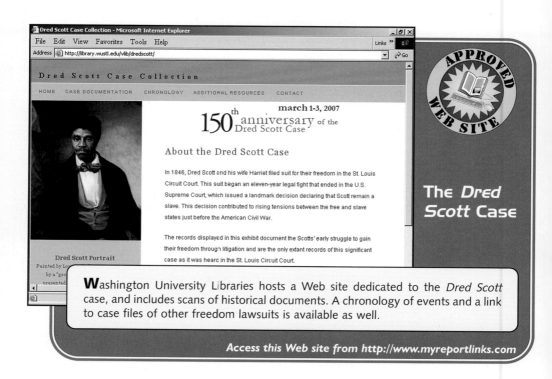

Washington University Libraries hosts a Web site dedicated to the *Dred Scott* case, and includes scans of historical documents. A chronology of events and a link to case files of other freedom lawsuits is available as well.

Access this Web site from http://www.myreportlinks.com

▲ *In April 1846, Dred Scott, a slave who had lived in Minnesota, a free state, sued Irene Emerson, who owned him, arguing that he should be freed. The United States Supreme Court ruled that Scott was neither free nor a citizen. Perhaps even worse, the court found that Scott had no right to sue.*

of calming tensions, the case had the effect of dumping gasoline on an already raging fire.

Dred Scott was a slave purchased by Dr. John Emerson in about 1833. Emerson, a surgeon in the Army, served in Illinois, a free state; in theory, if the laws of Illinois applied to Scott, he could be freed. In 1836, Emerson was relocated to what is now Minnesota, another free territory as determined by the Missouri Compromise. In May 1836, when Emerson was transferred to Fort Snelling in the newly created Wisconsin Territory, he took Scott with him. While in Wisconsin, Scott met and married the slave Harriet Robinson. Marriage was a legally-binding contract that did not apply to southern slaves.

The African American: A Journey From Slavery to Freedom

Long Island University presents this Web site dedicated to the history of slavery in the United States. You will find information on the establishment of slavery, the antislavery movement, important events, and key people involved during this period.

EDITOR'S CHOICE

Access this Web site from http://www.myreportlinks.com

When Emerson moved to St. Louis, Missouri, in 1837, he left Scott and his wife behind. Soon after he arrived in St. Louis, Emerson was transferred again, this time to Fort Jesup, Louisiana. When he arrived there on November 22, 1837, he sent for Scott and his wife.

In December 1843, Emerson died suddenly. Scott and his family were hired out for the next three years by Irene Emerson. In February 1846, Scott tried to buy his freedom from Emerson, but she refused to grant Scott's request. In April 1846, he sued, arguing that since he had lived in both a free state and a free territory, he had become legally free, and he could not have reverted to being a slave. The Supreme Court, under Chief Justice Roger B. Taney, held that Africans residing in America, whether slave or free, could not become U.S. citizens. Therefore, Dred Scott had no right to file a lawsuit. Furthermore, the Supreme Court declared that the parts of the Missouri Compromise creating free territories were unconstitutional because Congress had no authority to abolish slavery in federal territories.[10]

➡A Divided Union

Instead of relieving tensions between abolitionists and slavery advocates, the *Dred Scott* decision solidified the disagreements between the two sides. The Democratic party split, which allowed

In 1846, the Supreme Court, led by Chief Justice Roger Taney ruled in the Dred Scott case that Africans living in America could not become citizens. Observers had hoped the case would ease tensions between pro- and antislavery advocates, but it only worsened them.

American Civil War History Timelines Battle Map Pictures – Microsoft Internet Explorer

File   Edit   View   Favorites   Tools   Help   Links »

Address http://americancivilwar.com/   Go

American Civil War . com

This Site Sponsored in part by
March Through Times
March Through Times
Collectable toy soldiers
Volcano-Pictures.INFO
Native American
Bookstore

Civil War Video Games

Visit our Civil War Store

Kindle Books
Electronic Civil War Titles

AltaVista
Babel Fish
To translate this page, click a flag!

History Channel

THE HISTORY CHANNEL

Featured.Indexes
Summary Of Events
Civil War Timeline
State Battle Maps
Battles By Campaign
Naval Ships and Battles
Alphabetic Battle List
Colored Troops
Civil Wa
Tales of

AmericanCivilWar.com

People
Abraham Linc
Jefferson Davi
Ulysses S. Gra
Stonewall Jack
George B. Mc
General John F
General Rober

Done, but w

American Civil War

Biographies of key Civil War figures, casualty statistics, photographs, overviews of battles, timelines, and Civil War documents, are all available on this site. Suggestions for further reading and a section for young people are included.

Access this Web site from http://www.myreportlinks.com

APPROVED WEB SITE

the Republican party under Abraham Lincoln to sweep into power. Southern fears that the Republicans would abolish slavery caused a number of states to secede. Between December 20, 1860, and February 1, 1861, seven states—South Carolina, Mississippi, Florida, Alabama, Georgia, Louisiana, and Texas—left the Union and formed the Confederate States of America. After President Lincoln called for troops to stop the rebellion, four more states—Virginia, Arkansas, Tennessee, and North Carolina—joined the Confederacy.

A few states were split over whether to side with the North or South; they became known as "border states." Kentucky and Missouri were slave states that were technically admitted to the new Confederate States of America, but because they also had pro-Union governments, the Confederacy never really had any control over them. Maryland and Delaware were the other two slave states. Delaware rejected secession outright. Maryland rejected secession as well, but only after martial law had been imposed in order to stop riots in Baltimore. Torn between the two sides, Maryland contributed troops to both Northern and Southern armies during the war. Union-sympathizing counties in western Virginia then seceded from the State of Virginia. These counties formed West Virginia, which would initially be a slave state. However, its constitution gradually abolished slavery in the state.

→WAR BREAKS OUT

On April 12, 1861, a Confederate cannon in Charleston, South Carolina fired on the federal garrison at Fort Sumter, officially beginning the Civil War. Initially, the Confederate States of America won a number of major battles, including First Bull Run, the Peninsular Campaign, and the Second Battle of Bull Run. Confederate General Robert E. Lee then invaded Maryland, a state that Lee and other Confederate leaders felt would join the Confederacy. Lee's Army of Northern Virginia met the Union's Army of the Potomac, led by General

▲ Robert E. Lee was a career officer in the U.S. Army. Forced to choose between North and South when the Civil War erupted, he chose the South (remaining loyal to his native state of Virginia). It was his army that lost at Antietam.

George B. McClellan, at the Battle of Antietam, near Sharpsburg, Maryland, on September 17, 1862. Though Lee's forces were driven out of Maryland, McClellan made a major tactical error by failing to destroy the Confederates on the battlefield, and by not following Lee's army as it retreated to Virginia.[11]

Though Lincoln had wanted to issue the Emancipation Proclamation earlier than he did, he felt he needed to wait until the Union Army won a major battle. Antietam gave him the win he needed.

The Emancipation Proclamation freed all slaves in the Confederate States not already under Union control, though it did not free slaves in any Union states. Initially, the Civil War had been justified as necessary to maintain the United States as a single country. Lincoln's Emancipation Proclamation provided citizens with a moral reason for fighting the war.

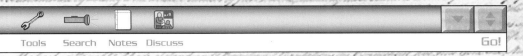
THE NEW AMENDMENTS

3

After Antietam, the Civil War dragged on for another two bloody, brutal years before it became apparent that the Union forces would defeat the Confederacy. In the meantime, abolitionists drafted an amendment to the constitution that would permanently outlaw slavery in the United States: the Thirteenth Amendment was proposed on January 31, 1865. Northern states quickly ratified the amendment. After the South surrendered on April 9, 1865, the Confederate States of America ceased to exist. And on December 6, 1865, after Georgia became the twenty-seventh state to ratify the Thirteenth Amendment, it became law.

⊖THE THIRTEENTH AMENDMENT

The Thirteenth Amendment is short and specifically worded, intended to prohibit slavery in the United States. Unlike most amendments to the Constitution, which list and define personal liberties, the language

The Civil War lasted almost five years and led to the death of more than 600,000 people. It remains the deadliest conflict in our history. But the United States emerged from this dark chapter a better and stronger society, with a brighter future for some its most oppressed members.

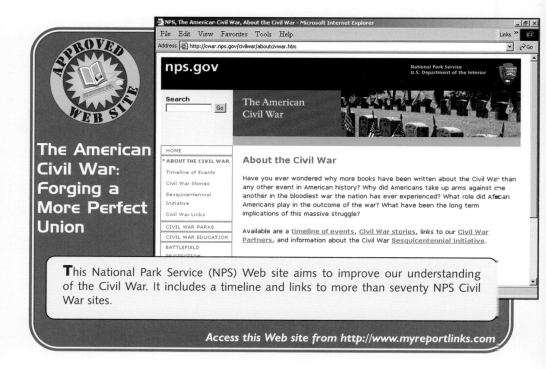

The American Civil War: Forging a More Perfect Union

NPS, The American Civil War, About the Civil War - Microsoft Internet Explorer

File   Edit   View   Favorites   Tools   Help   Links »

Address [http://cwar.nps.gov/civilwar/aboutcivwar.htm]   Go

nps.gov   National Park Service
                                 U.S. Department of the Interior

Search   The American
         [ ] Go   Civil War

HOME

+ ABOUT THE CIVIL WAR   **About the Civil War**

Timeline of Events   Have you ever wondered why more books have been written about the Civil War than
Civil War Stories   any other event in American history? Why did Americans take up arms against one
Sesquicentennial   another in the bloodiest war the nation has ever experienced? What role did African
Initiative   Americans play in the outcome of the war? What have been the long term
Civil War Links   implications of this massive struggle?

CIVIL WAR PARKS   Available are a timeline of events, Civil War stories, links to our Civil War
CIVIL WAR EDUCATION   Partners, and information about the Civil War Sesquicentennial Initiative.
BATTLEFIELD
PROTECTION

This National Park Service (NPS) Web site aims to improve our understanding of the Civil War. It includes a timeline and links to more than seventy NPS Civil War sites.

Access this Web site from http://www.myreportlinks.com

of the Thirteenth Amendment is limiting, expressly making certain actions illegal.

Section 1. Neither slavery nor involuntary servitude, except as a punishment for crime whereof the party shall have been duly convicted, shall exist within the United States, or any place subject to their jurisdiction.

This language specifically outlaws slavery or any form of involuntary servitude anywhere within the United States of America.

→ RECONSTRUCTION

After the Civil War ended, the United States entered the Reconstruction Era. Reconstruction was a period during which the federal government worked to reintegrate the rebellious Southern states back into the Union. During this time, African Americans in those states were able to vote and, because anyone who had been an elected official in the Confederacy was forbidden to participate in government, many African Americans were elected to Congress. But when Reconstruction ended in 1877 and the former representatives of the Confederacy were allowed to return to positions of power, they immediately worked to undermine many of the advances African Americans had made during Reconstruction.

For example, each of the former slave states passed "Black Codes," which gave newly freed

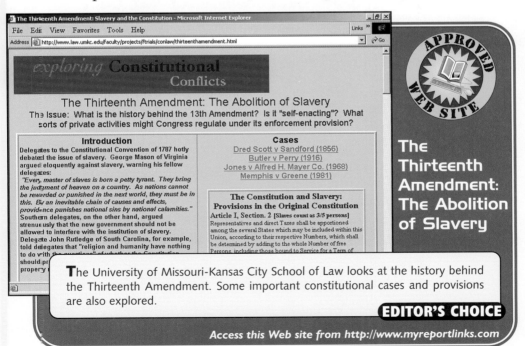

The University of Missouri-Kansas City School of Law looks at the history behind the Thirteenth Amendment. Some important constitutional cases and provisions are also explored.

EDITOR'S CHOICE

Access this Web site from http://www.myreportlinks.com

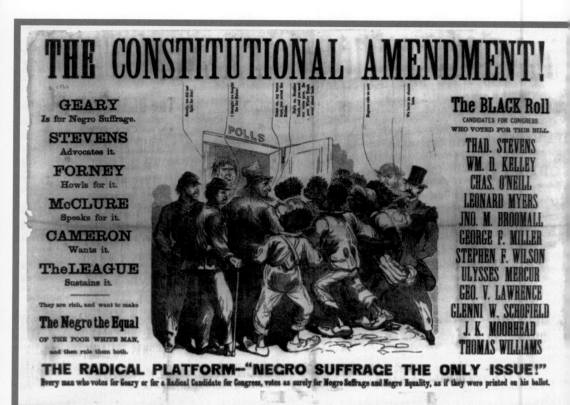

THE CONSTITUTIONAL AMENDMENT!

GEARY
Is for Negro Suffrage.

STEVENS
Advocates it.

FORNEY
Howls for it.

McCLURE
Speaks for it.

CAMERON
Wants it.

The LEAGUE
Sustains it.

They are rich, and want to make

The Negro the Equal
OF THE POOR WHITE MAN,
and then rule them both.

POLLS

The BLACK Roll
CANDIDATES FOR CONGRESS
WHO VOTED FOR THIS BILL.

THAD. STEVENS
WM. D. KELLEY
CHAS. O'NEILL
LEONARD MYERS
JNO. M. BROOMALL
GEORGE F. MILLER
STEPHEN F. WILSON
ULYSSES MERCUR
GEO. V. LAWRENCE
GLENNI W. SCHOFIELD
J. K. MOORHEAD
THOMAS WILLIAMS

THE RADICAL PLATFORM—"NEGRO SUFFRACE THE ONLY ISSUE!"
Every man who votes for Geary or for a Radical Candidate for Congress, votes as surely for Negro Suffrage and Negro Equality, as if they were printed on his ballot.

⚠ With the Thirteenth Amendment and the abolition of slavery came the right to vote, something many Americans did not support. After Reconstruction, the former slave states passed "Black Codes," laws that limited African Americans' civil rights and gave them no voting rights.

slaves few civil rights and no voting rights. Many northern legislators were infuriated, seeing these codes as nothing more than the South's refusal to accept that it had lost the war and that slavery had been abolished.

However, there was serious doubt as to whether Congress had jurisdiction over state legislatures and the right to pass laws to protect citizens' civil rights: In 1833, the U.S. Supreme

Court heard *Barron* v. *Baltimore,* and established the principle that the Bill of Rights only governed Federal, and not state, actions. In other words, at this stage of legal history, each individual state had the authority to determine what types of laws it passed, no matter what citizens in other states felt or believed.

→THE FOURTEENTH AMENDMENT

The Fourteenth Amendment was intended to give citizenship to all persons born or naturalized in the United States. This would grant citizenship to former slaves and overturn the *Dred Scott* v. *Sanford* decision. An important provision of the Amendment was the portion that said no state shall deprive any person of life, liberty, or property, without due process of law. A state also could not deny any person the equal protection of the law.

With these statements, the Amendment essentially cancelled the Black Codes. The new Fourteenth Amendment would apply due process of law, equal protection of the law, and the Bill of Rights to all state actions as well as federal ones. "In fact, the Bill of Rights did not become a vital instrument for the extension of civil liberties for anyone until after a bloody Civil War and a revolutionary Fourteenth Amendment intervened."[1]

The Amendment was proposed to Congress on June 13, 1866. Three days later, it was submitted to the states. On July 28, 1868, after the Fourteenth Amendment was ratified by the necessary twenty-eight, or three-quarters, of the thirty-seven states and became part of the U.S. Constitution.[2]

→FULL CITIZENSHIP

The Thirteenth Amendment outlawed the institution of slavery; the Fourteenth Amendment elevated African Americans, transforming them from "three-fifths" of one person to full-fledged citizens, eligible for many of the same Constitutional protections enjoyed by everyone else. With broad language that grants citizenship to virtually anyone born in the United States, the Fourteenth Amendment not only overturned the *Dred Scott* decision, but its due process and equal protection clauses were used in the 1950s to undercut the institution of segregation.

What follows is a more detailed look at each of the Amendment's clauses.

→SECTION ONE

Section One of the Fourteenth Amendment is legally the most important, as it ensures that the Bill of Rights applies to the state governments. Furthermore, this section provides a constitutional basis to support the idea that all American citizens are entitled to equal rights.

Section 1*. All persons born or naturalized in the United States, and subject to the jurisdiction thereof, are citizens of the United States and of the State wherein they reside. No State shall make or enforce any law which shall abridge the privileges or immunities of citizens of the United States; nor shall any State deprive any person of life, liberty, or property, without due process of law; nor deny to any person within its jurisdiction the equal protection of the laws.*

The first sentence of Section One is called the "citizenship clause." It essentially provides United

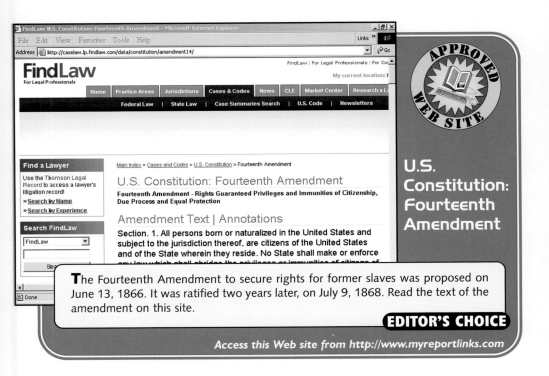

The Fourteenth Amendment to secure rights for former slaves was proposed on June 13, 1866. It was ratified two years later, on July 9, 1868. Read the text of the amendment on this site.

EDITOR'S CHOICE

Access this Web site from http://www.myreportlinks.com

The Fourteenth Amendment extended the due process clause to laws passed by state governments. The Fifth Amendment had previously established the due process clause to federal laws. The government can not take away liberty or property without fair trial or compensation.

States citizenship to virtually all people born on United States soil.

→ FIFTY-TWO WORDS

The second sentence, three clauses totaling fifty-two words, embodies a few of our country's most cherished ideals: the "privileges and immunities clause," the "due process clause" and the "equal protection clause."

The "privileges and immunities clause" applies the first eight amendments in the U.S. Bill of Rights to state actions as well as federal actions. The "due process clause" largely overshadows the privileges and immunities clause. It prevents the government from taking the life, freedom, or property of any United States citizen (including corporations) without the citizen having a fair chance to impact the outcome by a legal trial. While the Fifth Amendment does provide a right of due process, it had been interpreted to only mean federal government action. The Fourteenth Amendment applied the due process requirement to state governments as well.

Finally, the "equal protection clause" requires states to treat all citizens the same under the law.

→ SECTION TWO

Section 2. *Representatives shall be apportioned among the several States according to their respective* *numbers, counting the whole number of persons in each State, excluding Indians not taxed. But when the right to vote at any election for the choice of electors for President and Vice-President of the United States, Representatives in Congress, the Executive and Judicial officers of a State, or the members of the Legislature thereof, is denied to any of the male inhabitants of such State, being twenty-one years of age, and citizens of the United States, or in any way abridged, except for participation in rebellion, or other crime, the basis of representation therein shall be reduced in the proportion which the number of such male citizens shall bear to the whole number of male citizens twenty-one years of age in such State.*

Section Two of the Fourteenth Amendment overrides those sections of the Constitution that counted slaves as three-fifths of a person for state representation. Furthermore, Section Two punishes states that do not allow all eligible citizens to vote. It was initially intended to prevent states from denying the vote to newly freed African Americans. It established a penalty designed to ensure that men could vote: any time a male over age twenty-one was denied the vote, state representation would be decreased. In reality, however, this was never enforced, despite the fact that many southern states prevented African Americans from voting well into the 1960s.

THE AMENDMENTS AND THE LEGAL SYSTEM

4

In the American legal system, legal decisions are made based on cases that have already been decided. That is, if the Supreme Court hears a case today, it relies on decisions that it and other courts have already rendered in similar situations. Previous legal decisions are commonly referred to as "precedent" or "case law."

Case law of the Thirteenth and Fourteenth Amendments is often closely linked. The Thirteenth Amendment specifically prohibits slavery, but it relies on the more broadly worded and interpreted Fourteenth Amendment to enforce its jurisdiction over the states. The Fourteenth Amendment is more often cited as the reason why the Bill of Rights applies to all federal, state, and local government action. What follows is a closer look at some of the important Supreme Court cases dealing with the Thirteenth and Fourteenth Amendments.

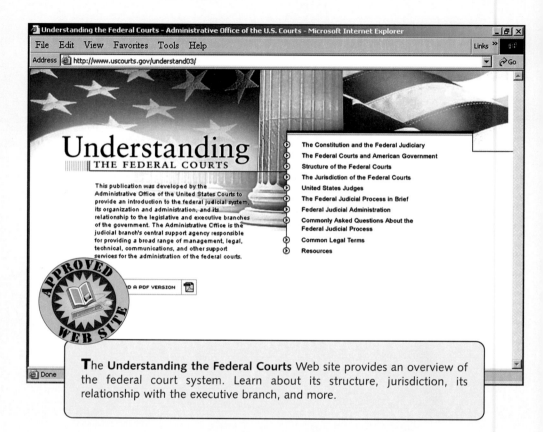

The **Understanding the Federal Courts** Web site provides an overview of the federal court system. Learn about its structure, jurisdiction, its relationship with the executive branch, and more.

→ THE SLAUGHTER-HOUSE CASES

The U.S. Supreme Court heard the first major challenge to the Fourteenth Amendment in 1873. The Slaughter-House cases, a group of three lawsuits that had been combined into one because they dealt with the same controversy, involved the state of Louisiana and slaughterhouses (where animals are killed and converted into food).

In 1869, the Louisiana legislature adopted a law that permitted the City of New Orleans to require slaughterhouses to be located in a single area. Several small independent butchers argued that the state was creating an unfair monopoly and shutting out independent butchers. The independent butchers sued, claiming Louisiana's action violated their due process rights and equal protection under the law.

The Supreme Court, under Chief Justice Salmon P. Chase, disagreed. He ruled that the Fourteenth Amendment does not protect the privileges and immunities of state citizenship, only the privileges and immunities of national citizenship. The privileges and immunities of state citizenship

This PBS Web site, **The Supreme Court: The First Hundred Years**, offers a brief summary of the court's history, biographies of Supreme Court Justices, and reviews of some landmark cases.

may not be interfered with by the Fourteenth Amendment's equal protection, due process, or privileges and immunities clauses.

STRAUDER V. WEST VIRGINIA

In 1873, Taylor Strauder was convicted of murdering his wife and sentenced to death. Strauder, an African American, was found guilty by a jury that was made up only of whites—under West Virginia law at the time, African Americans could not serve on a jury. Strauder appealed the verdict, arguing that excluding African Americans violated the equal protection clause. The Supreme Court, voting 7–2, upheld Strauder's appeal. Justice William Strong wrote:

> "Concluding, therefore, that the statute of West Virginia, discriminating in the selection of jurors, as it does, against negroes because of their color, amounts to a denial of the equal protection of the laws to a colored man when he is put upon trial for an alleged offence against the State. . . . "

He continued:

> . . . [The] Constitution . . . declares that 'all persons within the jurisdiction of the United States shall have the same right in every State and Territory to make and enforce contracts, to sue, be parties, give evidence, and to the full and equal benefit of all laws and proceedings for the security of persons and property, as is enjoyed by white citizens. . . .'[1]

In other words, the equal protection clause of the Fourteenth Amendment guaranteed that Strauder, and all African Americans, have a right to be tried by a racially-mixed jury.

→ THE CIVIL RIGHTS CASES

Strauder v. *West Virginia* established that the federal government can regulate how the Fourteenth Amendment is applied by state officials. But just a few years later, the Court heard another case which offered a slightly different interpretation of the Amendment and its reach.

Like the Slaughter-House cases heard previously, the *Civil Rights Cases* combined five similar

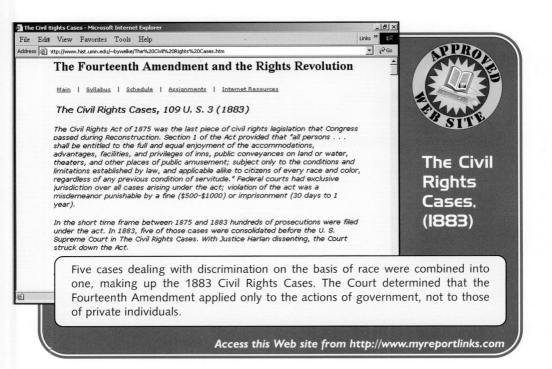

The Civil Rights Cases - Microsoft Internet Explorer

File   Edit   View   Favorites   Tools   Help   Links »

Address http://www.hist.umn.edu/~bywelke/The%20Civil%20Rights%20Cases.htm

The Fourteenth Amendment and the Rights Revolution

Main | Syllabus | Schedule | Assignments | Internet Resources

The Civil Rights Cases, 109 U. S. 3 (1883)

The Civil Rights Act of 1875 was the last piece of civil rights legislation that Congress passed during Reconstruction. Section 1 of the Act provided that "all persons . . . shall be entitled to the full and equal enjoyment of the accommodations, advantages, facilities, and privileges of inns, public conveyances on land or water, theaters, and other places of public amusement; subject only to the conditions and limitations established by law, and applicable alike to citizens of every race and color, regardless of any previous condition of servitude." Federal courts had exclusive jurisdiction over all cases arising under the act; violation of the act was a misdemeanor punishable by a fine ($500-$1000) or imprisonment (30 days to 1 year).

In the short time frame between 1875 and 1883 hundreds of prosecutions were filed under the act. In 1883, five of those cases were consolidated before the U. S. Supreme Court in The Civil Rights Cases. With Justice Harlan dissenting, the Court struck down the Act.

The Civil Rights Cases, (1883)

Five cases dealing with discrimination on the basis of race were combined into one, making up the 1883 Civil Rights Cases. The Court determined that the Fourteenth Amendment applied only to the actions of government, not to those of private individuals.

Access this Web site from http://www.myreportlinks.com

suits. In each case, African Americans had sued business owners who excluded them from private theaters, hotels, and transit companies. Each case argued that this violated the equal protection clause of the Fourteenth Amendment rights.

In a convincing 8–1 decision, the Court held that the equal protection clause only applies to the actions of the state and not actions undertaken by a privately-owned business. The Court also acknowledged that the Thirteenth Amendment applies to private individuals, but only to the extent that the amendment prohibits people from

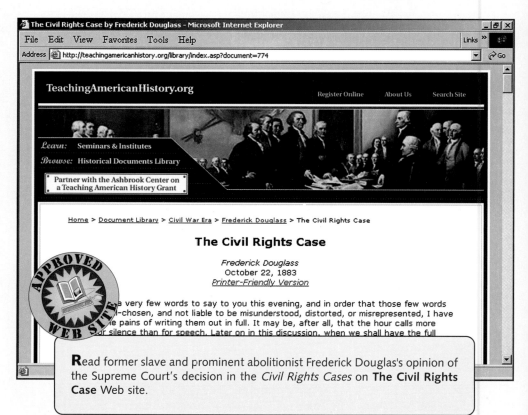

The Civil Rights Case by Frederick Douglass - Microsoft Internet Explorer

File   Edit   View   Favorites   Tools   Help   Links »

Address http://teachingamericanhistory.org/library/index.asp?document=774   Go

TeachingAmericanHistory.org   Register Online   About Us   Search Site

Learn: Seminars & Institutes
Browse: Historical Documents Library

Partner with the Ashbrook Center on
a Teaching American History Grant

Home > Document Library > Civil War Era > Frederick Douglass > The Civil Rights Case

The Civil Rights Case

Frederick Douglass
October 22, 1883
Printer-Friendly Version

...e very few words to say to you this evening, and in order that those few words
...-chosen, and not liable to be misunderstood, distorted, or misrepresented, I have
...e pains of writing them out in full. It may be, after all, that the hour calls more
...or silence than for speech. Later on in this discussion, when we shall have the full

Read former slave and prominent abolitionist Frederick Douglas's opinion of the Supreme Court's decision in the *Civil Rights Cases* on **The Civil Rights Case** Web site.

owning slaves; the amendment does not control whether individuals can exhibit discriminatory behavior. Justice Joseph P. Bradley wrote:

> "When a man has emerged from slavery . . . there must be some stage in the progress of his elevation when he takes the rank of a mere citizen, and ceases to be the special favorite of the laws . . . There were thousands of free colored people in this country before the abolition of slavery, enjoying all the essential rights of life, liberty, and property the same as white citizens; yet no one, at that time, thought that it was any invasion of their personal status as freemen because they were not admitted to all the privileges enjoyed by white citizens, or because they were subjected to discriminations in the enjoyment of accommodations in inns, public conveyances, and places of amusement. Mere discriminations on account of race or color were not regarded as badges of slavery. . . ."[2]

YICK WO V. HOPKINS

In 1880, the City of San Francisco passed an ordinance that said no laundromats could be operated in any wooden buildings without a permit from the Board of Supervisors. At the time, the vast majority of the city's laundries were located in wooden buildings, and, as it happened, the majority of these laundries were owned by Chinese immigrants. Most of those whom the ordinance affected applied for the required permit, but none were granted to Chinese owners. In contrast, only

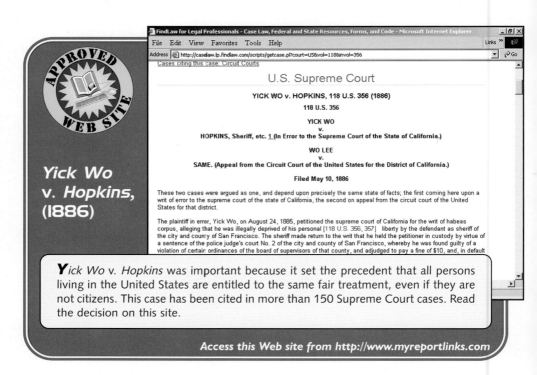

Yick Wo
v. Hopkins,
(1886)

FindLaw for Legal Professionals - Case Law, Federal and State Resources, Forms, and Code - Microsoft Internet Explorer

File   Edit   View   Favorites   Tools   Help

Address http://caselaw.lp.findlaw.com/scripts/getcase.pl?court=US&vol=118&invol=356

Cases citing this case: Circuit Courts

U.S. Supreme Court

YICK WO v. HOPKINS, 118 U.S. 356 (1886)

118 U.S. 356

YICK WO
v.
HOPKINS, Sheriff, etc. 1 (In Error to the Supreme Court of the State of California.)

WO LEE
v.
SAME. (Appeal from the Circuit Court of the United States for the District of California.)

Filed May 10, 1886

These two cases were argued as one, and depend upon precisely the same state of facts; the first coming here upon a writ of error to the supreme court of the state of California, the second on appeal from the circuit court of the United States for that district.

The plaintiff in error, Yick Wo, on August 24, 1885, petitioned the supreme court of California for the writ of habeas corpus, alleging that he was illegally deprived of his personal [118 U.S. 356, 357] liberty by the defendant as sheriff of the city and county of San Francisco. The sheriff made return to the writ that he held the petitioner in custody by virtue of a sentence of the police judge's court No. 2 of the city and county of San Francisco, whereby he was found guilty of a violation of certain ordinances of the board of supervisors of that county, and adjudged to pay a fine of $10, and, in default

Yick Wo v. Hopkins was important because it set the precedent that all persons living in the United States are entitled to the same fair treatment, even if they are not citizens. This case has been cited in more than 150 Supreme Court cases. Read the decision on this site.

Access this Web site from http://www.myreportlinks.com

one non-Chinese owner was denied a permit. Yick Wo, who had operated a laundry in a wooden building for many years, continued to run his business. He was convicted and fined for violating the San Francisco city ordinance.

Yick Wo carried his case to the U.S. Supreme Court, which found in 1886 that the law itself was not unconstitutional. But it ruled that the city's application of the law was unconstitutional. That is, the city enforced the regulation in a manner that was highly discriminatory, or unfair, to Chinese people. The Court declared that even immigrants who were not citizens could expect equal protection under the law. Justice Thomas Stanley Matthews wrote in the unanimous opinion:

> [The] consent of the supervisors is withheld from [the petitioners] . . . all of whom happen to be Chinese subjects, [while] eighty others, not Chinese subjects, are permitted to carry on the same business under similar conditions. . . . The fact of this discrimination is admitted. No reason for it is shown, and the conclusion cannot be resisted that no reason for it exists except hostility to the race and nationality to which the petitioners belong, and which, in the eye of the law, is not justified. The discrimination is therefore illegal, and the public administration which enforces it is a denial of the equal protection of the laws, and a violation of the fourteenth amendment of the constitution. . . .[3]

The Court's finding established the principle that virtually everyone is entitled to equal protection against discrimination; however, later case law rendered this finding largely irrelevant. It was almost another seventy years before the 1950s Warren Court cited *Yick Wo* v. *Hopkins* as the basis for striking down attempts to limit the rights of African Americans.

➔ *PLESSY V. FERGUSON*

On July 7, 1892, Homer Plessy took a seat on a railroad car reserved for white riders on the East

Louisiana Railroad. The thirty-year-old Plessy, who was one-eighth black and seven-eighths white, was arrested (Plessy had been selected to challenge the limits of the law by a group of citizens that was eager to challenge Louisiana's law). He had violated Louisiana's Separate Car Act, a law passed two years earlier that required separate cars for whites and blacks (the law also required that the separate facilities be "equal").

Eager to challenge Louisiana's "separate but equal" statute, the Citizen's Committee to Test the Separate Car Act raised money and hired a lawyer for Plessy, who argued that he had been denied his constitutional rights under the Thirteenth and

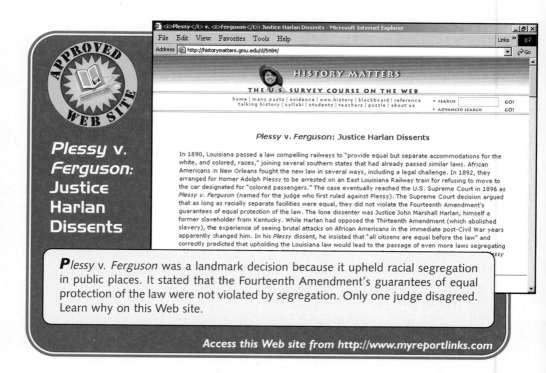

Plessy v. Ferguson: Justice Harlan Dissents

In 1890, Louisiana passed a law compelling railways to "provide equal but separate accommodations for the white, and colored, races," joining several southern states that had already passed similar laws. African Americans in New Orleans fought the new law in several ways, including a legal challenge. In 1892, they arranged for Homer Adolph Plessy to be arrested on an East Louisiana Railway train for refusing to move to the car designated for "colored passengers." The case eventually reached the U.S. Supreme Court in 1896 as *Plessy v. Ferguson* (named for the judge who first ruled against Plessy). The Supreme Court decision argued that as long as racially separate facilities were equal, they did not violate the Fourteenth Amendment's guarantees of equal protection of the law. The lone dissenter was Justice John Marshall Harlan, himself a former slaveholder from Kentucky. While Harlan had opposed the Thirteenth Amendment (which abolished slavery), the experience of seeing brutal attacks on African Americans in the immediate post-Civil War years apparently changed him. In his *Plessy* dissent, he insisted that "all citizens are equal before the law" and correctly predicted that upholding the Louisiana law would lead to the passage of even more laws segregating

**Plessy v. Ferguson:
Justice
Harlan
Dissents**

Plessy v. Ferguson was a landmark decision because it upheld racial segregation in public places. It stated that the Fourteenth Amendment's guarantees of equal protection of the law were not violated by segregation. Only one judge disagreed. Learn why on this Web site.

Access this Web site from http://www.myreportlinks.com

Fourteenth Amendments. A local Louisiana court denied the claim, as did the Louisiana Supreme Court. Plessy carried his case to the U.S. Supreme Court in 1896.

In a 7–1 decision in which one justice did not participate, the Court found that Plessy's Thirteenth Amendment rights had not been violated. The Court further found that Louisiana's law did not imply that African Americans were in any way inferior to whites, so the law did not violate the Fourteenth Amendment.

SEPARATE BUT EQUAL

In his majority opinion denying the Thirteenth Amendment claim, Justice Henry Billings Brown wrote:

> A statute which implies merely a legal distinction between the white and colored races . . . has no tendency to destroy the legal equality of the two races, or re-establish a state of involuntary servitude. . . .[4]

In other words, the Court found that because Plessy was not subjected to slavery or servitude, his Thirteenth Amendment rights were not violated.

In addressing Plessy's Fourteenth Amendment claim, Justice Brown wrote:

> The object of the amendment was undoubtedly to enforce the absolute equality of the two races

before the law, but, in the nature of things, it could not have been intended to abolish distinctions based upon color, or to enforce social, as distinguished from political, equality, or a commingling of the two races upon terms unsatisfactory to either. Laws permitting, and even requiring, their separation, in places where they are liable to be brought into contact, do not necessarily imply the inferiority of either race to the other, and have been generally, if not universally, recognized as within the competency of the state legislatures in the exercise of their police power. . . .[5]

Though the Court's ruling in *Plessy* did not establish the doctrine of "separate but equal," it strengthened the principle and provided legal cover for segregation, which had been going on since the end of the Civil War and Reconstruction. Even worse, the Supreme Court's decision firmly established "separate but equal" as the foundation on which Southern segregationists and racists built a legacy of hate and racial inequality that the legal community would not begin to undo for another fifty years.

→WHO'S A CITIZEN?

Though written and ratified as a response to the Civil War and the abolition of slavery, the Fourteenth Amendment's citizenship provisions also apply to other races.

Wong Kim Ark was born in San Francisco to Chinese parents (Ark was likely born around 1870, though there is no clear record of his birth). In 1890, Ark went to China to visit his parents, who had returned to their home country. When he returned to the United States, Ark was allowed to enter the country without any trouble. But five years later, after another visit to see his parents in China, Wong Kim Ark was not allowed to return to the United States.

CHINESE EXCLUSION ACT

In 1882, the United States enacted the Chinese Exclusion Act, a law intended to stop the large-scale immigration of Chinese into America. Over the years, further restrictions were put in place, making it more difficult for Chinese who had been in the United States to leave and reenter—which is why Wong Kim Ark was stopped at the Port of San Francisco in 1895. Ark sued, arguing that the wording of the Fourteenth Amendment made him a citizen.

The U.S. Supreme Court agreed and found that under the Fourteenth Amendment, a child born to foreign parents in the United States legally and who meet certain requirements, as Ark's parents did, is himself a citizen. The Court's ruling established a precedent that would have far-reaching

As a result of the Supreme Court's "separate but equal" finding in Plessy v. Ferguson, African Americans were forced to exist in a parallel world, one where public facilities like water fountains and restrooms could only be used by members of the same race.

impact on questions of citizenship. In his majority opinion, Justice Horace Gray wrote:

> The Fourteenth Amendment affirms the ancient and fundamental rule of citizenship by birth within the territory. . . . The amendment, in clear words and in manifest intent, includes the children born within the territory of the United States of all other persons, of whatever race or color, domiciled [living] within the United States. Every citizen or subject of another country, while domiciled here, is within the allegiance and the protection, and consequently subject to the jurisdiction, of the United States.[6]

BEREA COLLEGE V. KENTUCKY

While the Supreme Court demonstrated a precedent by forcing states to comply with the Fourteenth Amendment in *U.S.* v. *Wong Kim Ark,* its ruling in other cases made it clear that the Court was still hesitant to interfere with state government actions.

Berea College, a school in Kentucky, was founded in 1855. It admitted men and women, whites and blacks. In 1904, the Kentucky legislature passed a law designed to prevent blacks and whites from attending the same school. The law went so far as to forbid a school from teaching black and white students within twenty-five miles of each other. The law was clearly aimed at Berea College—it was the only integrated school in the state at the time. The school sued the state, losing locally before appealing to the U.S. Supreme Court.

In a ruling that at the time effectively legitimized segregation in public or private education, the Court held that states can legally prohibit private educational institutions chartered as corporations from admitting both black and white students. The Court held that while states may not be able to restrict the behavior of private individuals, states could legally prohibit private educational institutions chartered as corporations from admitting both black and white students.

➔ *GITLOW V. NEW YORK*

In the aftermath of World War I and the Russian Revolution (which led to the formation of the Soviet Union), people in the United States were very nervous about the spread of communism. So when Benjamin Gitlow, a Communist, sold thousands of copies of a radical newsletter called *The Left-Wing Manifesto* that advocated the overthrow of the government, he was arrested and charged with "criminal anarchy." Eventually, the State of New York convicted Gitlow for violating the New York Criminal Anarchy Law of 1902.

Gitlow took his case to the U.S. Supreme Court, which heard it in 1923. The Court under Chief Justice—and former President—William

Howard Taft upheld Gitlow's conviction. More important, Taft decided that the Fourteenth Amendment prohibited states from interfering with free speech, a First Amendment right of the United States Bill of Rights. Justice Edward Terry Sanford wrote in the majority opinion:

> For present purposes we may and do assume that freedom of speech and of the press—which are protected by the First Amendment from abridgment by Congress—are among the fundamental personal rights and 'liberties' protected by the due process clause of the Fourteenth Amendment from impairment by the States.[6]

Benjamin Gitlow's 1923 case against the State of New York concerned his First Amendment right to free speech. The Supreme Court's finding helped establish the principle that the Bill of Rights applied not just to federal government action, but to state and local government action, as well.

Gitlow v. *New York* was the first in a series of cases that reversed the 1833 decision in *Barron* v. *Baltimore,* where the Supreme Court had determined that the United States Bill of Rights could only be applied to federal governmental action, and not state actions. As a result of the *Gitlow* decision, courts began applying the Bill of Rights to all state and local government actions, establishing the modern legal view of the application of the Bill of Rights.[7]

⊜ SEPARATE BUT EQUAL SCHOOLS

The "separate but equal" doctrine established by *Plessy* v. *Ferguson* in 1896 was applied to schools in the 1927 case *Lum* v. *Rice.* Martha Lum was a nine-year-old girl of Chinese descent who lived in Mississippi. There were no schools for Chinese children in the area, so her parents tried to enroll her at the local white school. She was denied entrance. Gong Lum, Martha's father, sued; interestingly, his suit did not argue that discrimination based on race was illegal, but rather that officials had made an error when they classified his daughter as "colored."

The Supreme Court under Chief Justice William Howard Taft upheld the "separate but equal" doctrine established by *Plessy* and denied the Lum's claim. In the majority opinion, Taft wrote:

Most of the cases cited arose, it is true, over the establishment of separate schools as between white pupils and black pupils; but we cannot think that the question is any different, or that any different result can be reached, assuming the cases above cited to be rightly decided, where the issue is as between white pupils and the pupils of the yellow races. The decision is within the discretion of the state in regulating its public schools, and does not conflict with the Fourteenth Amendment.[8]

➔ *MISSOURI EX REL. GAINES V. CANADA*

The phrase "separate but equal" implies that a state that provides white students with an education must also provide schools for students of other races. In the 1938 case *Missouri ex rel. Gaines* v. *Canada,* the Supreme Court found that states must allow blacks and whites to attend the same school if there are no separate schools for blacks.

In 1936, the University of Missouri School of Law was the only public law school in the state. Lloyd Gaines was an African-American law student who was qualified to attend the Missouri law school. Gaines applied, but the school refused to admit him because he was black. While the state had plans to build a school for African Americans, it had yet to do so. Because the University of Missouri's law school was the only option available to Gaines, the Court found that:

The basic consideration is . . . what opportunities Missouri itself furnishes to white students and denies to negroes solely upon the ground of color. . . . The question here is not of a duty of the State to supply legal training, or of the quality of the training which it does supply, but of its duty when it provides such training to furnish it to the residents of the State upon the basis of an equality of right. By the operation of the laws of Missouri a privilege has been created for white law students which is denied to negroes by reason of their race. The white resident is afforded legal education within the State; the negro resident having the same qualifications is refused it there and must go outside the State to obtain it. That is a denial of the equality of legal right to the enjoyment of the privilege which the State has set up. . . ."[9]

This comprehensive Web site on African-American history features an online encyclopedia, timelines, primary documents, and speeches given by prominent African Americans between 1789 and 2004.

Access this Web site from http://www.myreportlinks.com

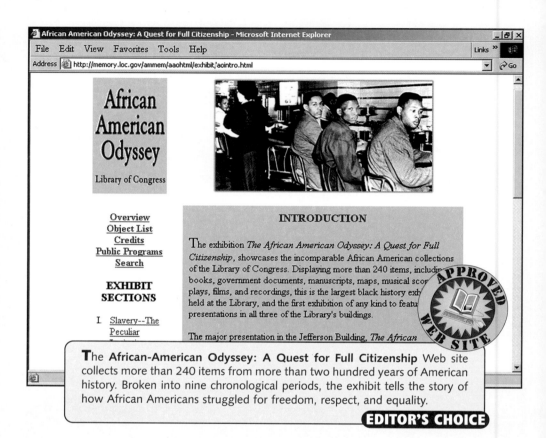

African American Odyssey: A Quest for Full Citizenship - Microsoft Internet Explorer

File   Edit   View   Favorites   Tools   Help   Links »

Address ⌐ http://memory.loc.gov/ammem/aaohtml/exhibit/aointro.html   ▼ ∂ Go

African American Odyssey

Library of Congress

Overview
Object List
Credits
Public Programs
Search

EXHIBIT SECTIONS

I. Slavery--The
    Peculiar

INTRODUCTION

The exhibition *The African American Odyssey: A Quest for Full Citizenship*, showcases the incomparable African American collections of the Library of Congress. Displaying more than 240 items, including books, government documents, manuscripts, maps, musical scores, plays, films, and recordings, this is the largest black history exhibit held at the Library, and the first exhibition of any kind to feature presentations in all three of the Library's buildings.

The major presentation in the Jefferson Building, *The African*

The **African-American Odyssey: A Quest for Full Citizenship** Web site collects more than 240 items from more than two hundred years of American history. Broken into nine chronological periods, the exhibit tells the story of how African Americans struggled for freedom, respect, and equality.

EDITOR'S CHOICE

⊛ *Edwards v. California*

In December 1939, a man named Edwards (whose first name does not appear in records) drove from his home in Marysville, California, to Spur, Texas. Edwards went to Texas to pick up his wife's brother, Frank Duncan, whom he would then drive back to California. Nothing out of the ordinary, except that Duncan was an "indigent person," meaning he was poor.

In 1939, the United States was still struggling with the Great Depression and the Dust Bowl, a period of severe drought that forced thousands of Midwest families to leave their homes and move to California, where they expected to find a better life. In 1937, in an attempt to slow the wave of poor people streaming into the state, California passed a law that made it a crime for anyone to knowingly bring a poor person into the state. Edwards violated this state law.

In *Edwards* v. *California,* the Supreme Court held that if a state government tries to prevent citizens from moving within a state or from one state to another, it can be a violation of the privileges and immunities clause of the Fourteenth Amendment. The Court struck down the California law, declaring that a state cannot prohibit poor people from moving into it.

➔ *SMITH* V. *ALLWRIGHT*

Historically, the Supreme Court steered clear of issues relating to private clubs or organizations and their membership. In other words, it generally rendered no opinion on a club's decision to admit whites only or deny admission to non-whites. This began to change in 1944, when the Court heard *Smith* v. *Allwright.*

Many Southern states, including Texas, where the *Smith* case began, claimed that the Democratic party was a private organization and could exclude anyone it wanted to—and it wanted to exclude non-whites from voting in the party primary elections. This effectively meant that many non-white voters would not have a chance to vote (the Republican party was both weak in the South at the time and not a realistic option for African Americans given the party's support during the twentieth century for segregation).

The Supreme Court did not agree with the Democratic Party's interpretation and found that all voters had to be allowed to participate in the primaries. Justice Stanley Foreman Reed stated:

> The privilege of membership in a party may be . . . no concern of a state. But when, as here, that privilege is also the essential qualification for voting in a primary to select nominees for a general election, the state makes the action of the party the action of the state.[10]

→ SHELLY V. KRAEMER

In 1945, an African-American family named Shelley bought a house in St. Louis, Missouri. Unknown to them, the deed to the property included a covenant (or an agreement) written in 1911 that that barred "people of the Negro or Mongolian Race" from owning the property. Neighborhood residents tried to prevent the Shelleys from taking possession of the property.

The Supreme Court took up the issue of property rights and the Fourteenth Amendment when

After all is said and done, it is left to the nine justices of the Supreme Court to determine what rights are protected by the First Amendment. This is the Supreme Court Building.

it agreed to hear *Shelley* v. *Kraemer* in 1948. The Court decided that racially-based, restrictive contracts were not in themselves a violation of the Fourteenth Amendment. However, it determined that these restrictions were absolutely unenforceable because state court action would be required to enforce them, and a state action enforcing a racially-based, restrictive covenant would be discriminatory and therefore prohibited by the Fourteenth Amendment.

⊖ EQUAL EDUCATION

By the mid-twentieth century, life in America was obviously better for African Americans than it had been a hundred years before. Still, there were plenty of arenas where whites worked hard to keep African Americans from making much real progress.

Despite being qualified, Heman Marion Sweatt, an African-American man, was denied admission to the University of Texas School of Law—the Texas state constitution banned integrated education. Rather than render a verdict, the trial court stalled for time as the state of Texas rushed to create a separate law school for non-whites. Sweatt appealed the lower court's actions first to the Court of Civil Appeals and then the Texas Supreme Court, both of which upheld the lower court. Sweatt, backed by the

National Association for the Advancement of Colored People (NAACP), appealed to the Supreme Court.

The Court found that there was a large difference between both the quality of the facilities and the quality of the education offered by the University of Texas School of Law and the new non-white law school. Because of this, the required "equal opportunity" that the state was supposed to provide didn't exist. Therefore, denying Sweatt admission to the stronger academic school was a violation of his Fourteenth Amendment rights. The Court ordered that Sweatt be admitted to the University of Texas School of Law. Chief Justice Fred M. Vinson wrote:

> . . . This Court has stated unanimously that 'The State must provide [legal education] for [petitioner] in conformity with the equal protection clause of the Fourteenth Amendment and provide it as soon as it does for applicants of any other group.' In accordance, petitioner may claim his full constitutional right: legal education equivalent to that offered by the State to students of other races. Such education is not available to him in a separate law school as offered by the State.[11]

➔ BEGINNING OF THE END

The decision in Sweatt set the stage for the end of the *Plessy* doctrine of "separate but equal" by recognizing the fact that the existence of a separate institution does not automatically confer equality. The real revolution came a few years later.

➔ BROWN V. BOARD OF EDUCATION

Linda Brown was no different than many other African-American students in America in the 1950s. Linda, a third-grader in Topeka, Kansas, had to walk a mile and then ride a bus to an all-black school about five miles from her house. Though there was another elementary school about five blocks from Linda Brown's house, it was for white students only. And when Oliver L. Brown tried to enroll his daughter at that nearby school, he was told she could not attend it.

But, Linda's father, Oliver, was determined to change things—and in 1951, he decided to sue the Topeka Board of Education, arguing that the "separate but equal" standard established in the 1896 *Plessy* v. *Ferguson* case perpetuated the inferior treatment of African Americans. Brown and the twelve other families who joined his suit, lost their case in Kansas' District Court. Supported by the NAACP and joined by plaintiffs from four other cases around the country, the U.S. Supreme Court heard *Brown* v. *Board of Education* in 1954. It remains one of the most important Supreme Court decisions in United States history.

In a strongly-worded unanimous decision, the Supreme Court eliminated the *Plessy* standard of

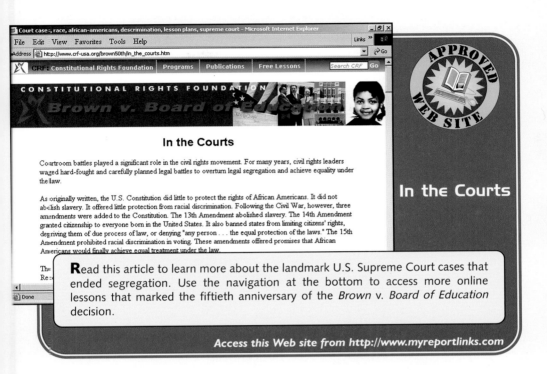

Court cases, race, african-americans, descrimination, lesson plans, supreme court - Microsoft Internet Explorer

File   Edit   View   Favorites   Tools   Help   Links »

Address http://www.crf-usa.org/brown50th/in_the_courts.htm   Go

CRF: Constitutional Rights Foundation   Programs   Publications   Free Lessons   Search CRF   Go

CONSTITUTIONAL RIGHTS FOUNDATION

Brown v. Board of Education

In the Courts

Courtroom battles played a significant role in the civil rights movement. For many years, civil rights leaders waged hard-fought and carefully planned legal battles to overturn legal segregation and achieve equality under the law.

As originally written, the U.S. Constitution did little to protect the rights of African Americans. It did not abolish slavery. It offered little protection from racial discrimination. Following the Civil War, however, three amendments were added to the Constitution. The 13th Amendment abolished slavery. The 14th Amendment granted citizenship to everyone born in the United States. It also banned states from limiting citizens' rights, depriving them of due process of law, or denying "any person . . . the equal protection of the laws." The 15th Amendment prohibited racial discrimination in voting. These amendments offered promises that African Americans would finally achieve equal treatment under the law.

In the Courts

Read this article to learn more about the landmark U.S. Supreme Court cases that ended segregation. Use the navigation at the bottom to access more online lessons that marked the fiftieth anniversary of the *Brown* v. *Board of Education* decision.

Access this Web site from http://www.myreportlinks.com

"separate but equal" stating that separate facilities for whites and non-whites was inherently unequal. Chief Justice Earl Warren wrote:

> . . . [Education] is the very foundation of good citizenship. Today it is a principal instrument in awakening the child to cultural values, in preparing him for later professional training, and in helping him to adjust normally to his environment. In these days, it is doubtful that any child may reasonably be expected to succeed in life if he is denied the opportunity of an education. Such an opportunity, where the state has undertaken to provide it, is a right which must be made available to all on equal terms.[12]

The Supreme Court's decision in 1954's Brown v. Board of Education case did not undo a century's worth of segregation, but it did destroy the principle of "separate but equal." Indeed, this decision was instrumental in opening the door to real racial integration.

The chief justice further stated,

> We conclude that in the field of public education the doctrine of 'separate but equal' has no place. Separate educational facilities are inherently unequal. Therefore, we hold that the plaintiffs . . . are, by reason of the segregation complained of, deprived of the equal protection of the laws guaranteed by the Fourteenth Amendment.[13]

The *Brown* v. *Board of Education* decision opened the door to real racial integration, but it did not immediately and miraculously end segregation or racial discrimination in America. However, it destroyed "separate but equal" and helped ignite what would soon become known as the Civil Rights Movement.

→ GIDEON V. WAINWRIGHT

In June 1961, Clarence Earl Gideon was arrested and charged with breaking and entering a pool hall in Panama City, Florida. Gideon was too poor to afford an attorney, and though he asked the court to appoint one for him, the request was denied—the judge in his case ruled that only poor defendants in murder cases or where "special circumstances" existed were entitled to free counsel. Gideon, forced to act as his own lawyer, was found guilty and sentenced to five years in jail.

While he was in prison, Gideon studied law and he eventually filed a motion with the

▲ *Clarence Earl Gideon was convicted of breaking and entering in 1961. He appealed, arguing that his Fourteenth Amendment due process rights had been violated because he had been denied counsel. The Court agreed, thus establishing the principle that all defendants are entitled to counsel.*

Supreme Court of Florida. When his petition with the state was denied, he handwrote a petition to the U.S. Supreme Court, naming Louie L. Wainwright, the Secretary to the Florida Department of Corrections, as the defendant. The Court agreed to hear his case.

Gideon strongly argued that his Fourteenth Amendment due process rights had been violated because he was denied counsel. The Warren Court agreed, specifically overturning a previous decision it had made in a similar case in 1942. Justice Hugo Black wrote:

"... [W]e ... restore constitutional principles established to achieve a fair system of justice. . . [R]eason and reflection require us to recognize that in our adversary system of criminal justice, any person hauled into court, who is too poor to hire a lawyer, cannot be assured a fair trial unless counsel is provided for him. . . . That government hires lawyers to prosecute and defendants who have the money hire lawyers to defend are the strongest indications of the widespread belief that lawyers in criminal courts are necessities, not luxuries. The right of one charged with crime to counsel may not be deemed fundamental and essential to fair trials in some countries, but it is in ours. . . . This noble ideal cannot be realized if the poor man charged with crime has to face his accusers without a lawyer to assist him.[14]

A RARE DECISION

The Court's decision in *Gideon* was noteworthy for a few reasons. First, it was one of the rare times when the Supreme Court reversed earlier Court decisions to establish new legal precedent. But even more than that, by asserting that all defendants, regardless of wealth or education, were entitled to the benefit of counsel, the decision greatly expanded the system of public defenders that now exists.

➡ LOVING V. VIRGINIA

In June 1958, Mildred Jeter and Richard Perry Loving left their home in Virginia and went to Washington, D.C., to get married. Jeter, an African-American woman, and Loving, a white man, were trying to work around Virginia's Racial Integrity Act, which made interracial marriage illegal. When the newly-married couple returned to their home in Virginia, they were arrested.

The couple was charged with violating the statute and on January 6, 1959, they pled guilty and were sentenced to one year in prison. However, the state agreed to suspend the sentence on the condition that the pair left the state of Virginia.

The Lovings agreed and moved to Washington, D.C. But in November 1963, they went to court to have Virginia's ruling thrown out—the Lovings argued that it violated the due process clause of the Fourteenth Amendment.

In 1967, the Warren Court unanimously decided that the Virginia law was unconstitutional. Chief Justice Warren wrote:

> These statutes also deprive the Lovings of liberty without due process of law in violation of the Due

Married in Washington, D.C., in June 1958, Mildred and Richard Loving were arrested soon after they returned home to Virginia. Finally, on June 12, 1967, the Supreme Court upheld the right for them and all interracial couples to wed.

Process Clause of the Fourteenth Amendment. The freedom to marry has long been recognized as one of the vital personal rights essential to the orderly pursuit of happiness by free men.

Marriage is one of the "basic civil rights of man." . . . To deny this fundamental freedom on so unsupportable a basis as the racial classifications embodied in these statutes . . . is surely to deprive all the State's citizens of liberty without due process of law. Under our Constitution, the freedom to marry, or not marry, a person of another race resides with the individual and cannot be infringed by the State.[15]

GOLDBERG V. KELLY

In 1968, residents of New York City who had been receiving financial aid from New York state's Home Relief program or money from the Aid to Families with Dependent Children were told they would no longer receive assistance. A group of citizens filed suit in District Court, arguing that by making this decision without public discussion or prior notice, New York state had violated the due process clause of the Fourteenth Amendment.

The Supreme Court under Chief Justice Warren Burger decided that government aid programs, also known as welfare or entitlements, are a form of a property right. Therefore, the entitlements were governed by the due process clause. Justice William J. Brennan wrote:

". . . [I]mportant governmental interests are promoted by affording recipients a pre-termination evidentiary hearing. From its founding the Nation's basic commitment has been to foster the dignity and well-being of all persons within its borders. We have come to recognize that forces not within the control of the poor contribute to their poverty . . . Welfare, by meeting the basic demands of subsistence, can help bring within the reach of the poor the same opportunities that are available to others to participate meaningfully in the life of the community. Public assistance, then, is not mere charity, but a means to 'promote the general Welfare, and secure the Blessings of Liberty to ourselves and our Posterity.' The same governmental interests that counsel the provision of welfare, counsel as well its uninterrupted provision to those eligible to receive it; pre-termination evidentiary hearings are indispensable. . . ."[16]

It should be noted that Justice Brennan did not think a full trial was necessary to satisfy due process; an administrative review where a "fair hearing" was possible would be sufficient. Nonetheless, someone on welfare would need notice before their payments ended.

⊖ MISSISSIPPI UNIVERSITY FOR WOMEN V. HOGAN

In 1979, male nurse Joe Hogan applied to the Mississippi University for Women's four-year degree program in nursing. Though he was qualified,

◀ *Sandra Day O'Connor served on the Supreme Court from 1981 to 2006. She was the first woman to serve on the Court.*

Hogan was obviously denied admission. Hogan sued, arguing that the nursing school's single-sex admission policy violated the equal protection clause of the Fourteenth Amendment.

Justice Sandra Day O'Connor tried to determine whether a state program that discriminates against a group of citizens serves important governmental objectives. She also needed to determine whether the discrimination in question plays any role in the program's ability to achieve its goals. In other words, did the school *need* to exclude men from admission in order to be able to teach women to become nurses? She wrote:

> Although the test for determining the validity of a gender-based classification is straightforward, it must be applied free of fixed notions concerning the roles and abilities of males and females. Care

must be taken in ascertaining whether the statutory objective itself reflects archaic and stereotypic notions. Thus, if the statutory objective is to exclude or 'protect' members of one gender because they are presumed to suffer from an inherent handicap or to be innately inferior, the objective itself is illegitimate.[17]

In other words, if an institution deliberately favored one gender, it would not be equally protecting both genders. Such an action would be a violation of the equal protection clause of the Fourteenth Amendment.

Ultimately, Justice O'Connor determined that the Mississippi school violated Hogan's rights: The school was keeping men out of a women's school on the grounds that women would be adversely affected by the men being there. The school, however, failed to prove that single-sex classes were necessary to maintain a quality education for it's students.

5   MODERN SLAVERY

While slavery is not often regarded as a contemporary issue, it remains a major world problem, just under a different name. "Trafficking" or human trafficking is a form of modern-day slavery that involves acquiring and transporting people with the intention of forcing them to do something they do not want to do. According to recent U.S. government estimates, eighteen to twenty-thousand persons are trafficked into the United States each year for purposes of sexual exploitation or forced labor. The problem is much larger worldwide.

⊖ *UNITED STATES V. KOZMINSKI*

Almost 125 years after President Lincoln issued the Emancipation Proclamation abolishing slavery, the Supreme Court was forced to revisit issues relating to forced labor, or enslavement.

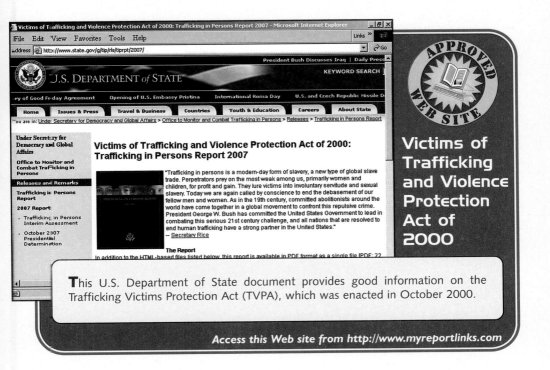

Victims of Trafficking and Violence Protection Act of 2000: Trafficking in Persons Report 2007 – Microsoft Internet Explorer

File   Edit   View   Favorites   Tools   Help

address http://www.state.gov/g/tip/rls/tiprpt/2007/

President Bush Discusses Iraq | Daily Press

U.S. DEPARTMENT of STATE

KEYWORD SEARCH

ry of Good Friday Agreement   Opening of U.S. Embassy Pristina   International Roma Day   U.S. and Czech Republic Missile D

Home | Issues & Press | Travel & Business | Countries | Youth & Education | Careers | About State

ou are in: Under Secretary for Democracy and Global Affairs > Office to Monitor and Combat Trafficking in Persons > Releases > Trafficking in Persons Report

Under Secretary for Democracy and Global Affairs

Office to Monitor and Combat Trafficking in Persons

Releases and Remarks

Trafficking in Persons Report

2007 Report
- Trafficking in Persons Interim Assessment
- October 2007 Presidential Determination

Victims of Trafficking and Violence Protection Act of 2000: Trafficking in Persons Report 2007

"Trafficking in persons is a modern-day form of slavery, a new type of global slave trade. Perpetrators prey on the most weak among us, primarily women and children, for profit and gain. They lure victims into involuntary servitude and sexual slavery. Today we are again called by conscience to end the debasement of our fellow men and women. As in the 19th century, committed abolitionists around the world have come together in a global movement to confront this repulsive crime. President George W. Bush has committed the United States Government to lead in combating this serious 21st century challenge, and all nations that are resolved to end human trafficking have a strong partner in the United States."
– Secretary Rice

The Report
In addition to the HTML-based files listed below, this report is available in PDF format as a single file (PDF: 22

Victims of Trafficking and Violence Protection Act of 2000

This U.S. Department of State document provides good information on the Trafficking Victims Protection Act (TVPA), which was enacted in October 2000.

Access this Web site from http://www.myreportlinks.com

In the 1980s, two mentally-challenged men were found working on a farm in Kentucky. Not only were the two men sometimes forced to work seventeen hours per day, seven days per week, they lived in horrible conditions. Finally, the men were threatened, either with physical abuse or by being told that they would be institutionalized if they did not do as they were told.

The farm operators were charged with conspiring to prevent the men from exercising their Thirteenth Amendment right to be free from involuntary servitude. The Supreme Court asserted that "involuntary servitude" necessarily means a condition of servitude in which the victim is forced

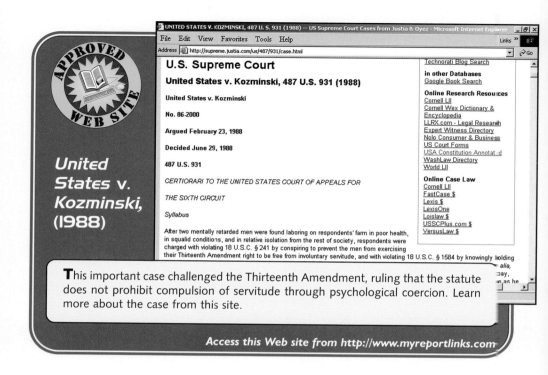

UNITED STATES V. KOZMINSKI, 487 U. S. 931 (1988) -- US Supreme Court Cases from Justia & Oyez - Microsoft Internet Explorer

File   Edit   View   Favorites   Tools   Help   Links »

Address | http://supreme.justia.com/us/487/931/case.html | ʔGo

U.S. Supreme Court

United States v. Kozminski, 487 U.S. 931 (1988)

United States v. Kozminski

No. 86-2000

Argued February 23, 1988

Decided June 29, 1988

487 U.S. 931

CERTIORARI TO THE UNITED STATES COURT OF APPEALS FOR

THE SIXTH CIRCUIT

Syllabus

After two mentally retarded men were found laboring on respondents' farm in poor health, in squalid conditions, and in relative isolation from the rest of society, respondents were charged with violating 18 U.S.C. § 241 by conspiring to prevent the men from exercising their Thirteenth Amendment right to be free from involuntary servitude, and with violating 18 U.S.C. § 1584 by knowingly holding

Technorati Blog Search

in other Databases
Google Book Search

Online Research Resources
Cornell LII
Cornell Wex Dictionary &
Encyclopedia
LLRX.com - Legal Research
Expert Witness Directory
Nolo Consumer & Business
US Court Forms
USA Constitution Annotated
WashLaw Directory
World LII

Online Case Law
Cornell LII
FastCase $
Lexis $
LexisOne
Loislaw $
USSCPlus.com $
VersusLaw $

This important case challenged the Thirteenth Amendment, ruling that the statute does not prohibit compulsion of servitude through psychological coercion. Learn more about the case from this site.

Access this Web site from http://www.myreportlinks.com

United States v. Kozminski, (1988)

to work for a defendant by the use or threat of physical restraint, physical injury, or by the use or threat of coercion through law or the legal process. This definition includes cases in which the defendant holds the victim in servitude by placing him or her in fear of such physical restraint or injury or legal coercion (in *Kozminski,* that element of coercion was absent or at least unproven).

Justice O'Connor wrote:

Our precedents clearly define a Thirteenth Amendment prohibition of involuntary servitude enforced by the use or threatened use of physical or legal coercion. The guarantee of freedom from involuntary servitude has never been interpreted specifically to prohibit compulsion of labor by other means, such as psychological coercion. We draw no conclusions from this historical survey about the potential scope of the Thirteenth Amendment. Viewing the Amendment, however, through the narrow window that is appropriate, . . . it is clear that the Government cannot prove a conspiracy to violate rights secured by the Thirteenth Amendment without proving that the conspiracy involved the use or threatened use of physical or legal coercion.[1]

In other words, the Court determined that government could not prove that the operators in *Kozminski* had either used force or threatened to

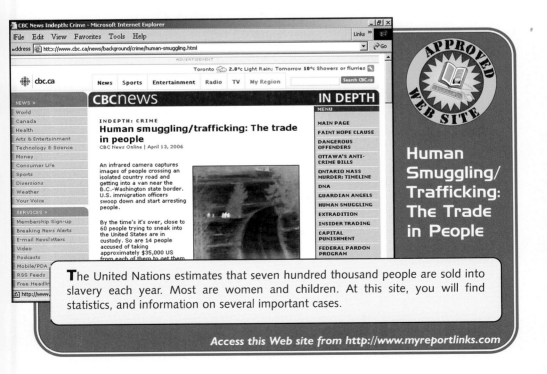

The United Nations estimates that seven hundred thousand people are sold into slavery each year. Most are women and children. At this site, you will find statistics, and information on several important cases.

Access this Web site from http://www.myreportlinks.com

use force to control the men who worked for them. Therefore, the operators were not guilty of violating the workers' Thirteenth Amendment rights. Up to that point, Congress had not made other forms of coercion illegal.

But the Court's decision prompted Congress to act. In October 2000, it passed the Trafficking Victims Protection Act (TVPA), the most comprehensive U.S. law to address the various criminal aspects of the human trafficking industry both internationally and domestically.

→ DISCRIMINATION IN MANY FORMS

Unfortunately, discrimination issues are still at the forefront of the legal agenda. But discrimination

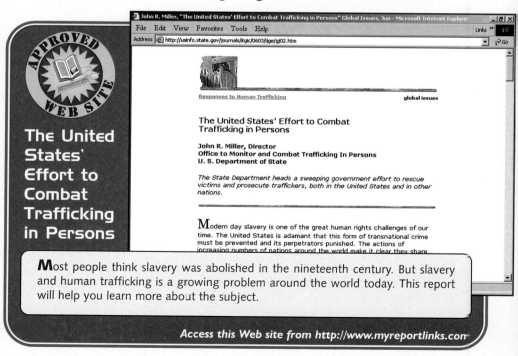

APPROVED WEB SITE

The United States' Effort to Combat Trafficking in Persons

John R. Miller, "The United States' Effort to Combat Trafficking in Persons" Global Issues, Jun - Microsoft Internet Explorer

File   Edit   View   Favorites   Tools   Help   Links »

Address http://usinfo.state.gov/journals/itgic/0603/ijge/gj02.htm   Go

Responses to Human Trafficking   global issues

The United States' Effort to Combat Trafficking in Persons

John R. Miller, Director
Office to Monitor and Combat Trafficking In Persons
U. S. Department of State

The State Department heads a sweeping government effort to rescue victims and prosecute traffickers, both in the United States and in other nations.

Modern day slavery is one of the great human rights challenges of our time. The United States is adamant that this form of transnational crime must be prevented and its perpetrators punished. The actions of increasing numbers of nations around the world make it clear they share

Most people think slavery was abolished in the nineteenth century. But slavery and human trafficking is a growing problem around the world today. This report will help you learn more about the subject.

Access this Web site from http://www.myreportlinks.com

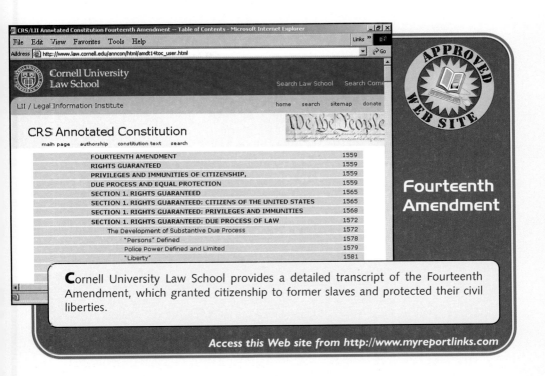

Fourteenth Amendment

Cornell University Law School provides a detailed transcript of the Fourteenth Amendment, which granted citizenship to former slaves and protected their civil liberties.

Access this Web site from http://www.myreportlinks.com

issues have expanded well beyond race to include gender and sexual preference cases as well. These cases rely on the broad wording the Fourteenth Amendment and look to it to protect the rights of all Americans—black, white, gay, or straight.

UNITED STATES V. VIRGINIA

In 1996, the Supreme Court held that the State of Virginia could not exclude women from the Virginia Military Institute (VMI), stating that the school's policy violated the equal protection clause of the Fourteenth Amendment.

The Virginia Military Institute was an all-male state-funded military academy. When some

▲ *Gussie Ann Lord (above), a former cheerleader, became one of the first twenty-three women to earn recognition as a full cadet at the Virginia Military Institute after the U.S. Supreme Court ruled in 1996 that the school's all-male admission policy violated the Equal Protection Clause of the Fourteenth Amendment.*

women applied for admission, the state offered to set up a separate but equal program on another college campus that it would call the Virginia Women's Institute for Leadership (VWIL). The Supreme Court rejected the state's contention that the VWIL education would be equivalent to a VMI education. Further, the Court said the state had not provided any legitimate reason why it should be allowed to discriminate against women and violate of the Fourteenth Amendment.

Justice Ruth Bader Ginsburg wrote:

> VMI, too, offers an educational opportunity no other Virginia institution provides . . . [and] Virginia has closed this facility to its daughters and, instead, has devised for them a 'parallel program,' with a faculty less impressively credentialed and less well paid, more limited course offerings, fewer opportunities for military training and for scientific specialization. VMI, beyond question, 'possesses to a far greater degree' than the VWIL program 'those qualities which are incapable of objective measurement but which make for greatness in a . . . school' . . . Women seeking and fit for a VMI-quality education cannot be offered anything less, under the State's obligation to afford them genuinely equal protection.

> A prime part of the history of our Constitution . . . is the story of the extension of constitutional rights and protections to people once ignored or excluded. . . . There is no reason to believe that the admission of women capable of all the activities required of VMI cadets would destroy the Institute rather than enhance its capacity to serve the 'more perfect Union.'[2]

➔SAME-SEX MARRIAGE

The marriage equality movement for same-sex marriages is starting to rely on the precedents based on the equal protection claims set in *Loving* v. *Virginia*, as a basis of legality. Some states have taken steps to allow same-sex marriage. On the state level, by 2008 both California and Massachusetts have legalized same-sex marriage with some resistance. Other states, such as Vermont, New Jersey, Connecticut, and New Hampshire have granted homosexual couples "civil unions" in which the couples have many of the same rights as straight couples. Meanwhile, many states have passed amendments to their state constitutions banning same-sex marriages in their states.

On September 21, 1996, the United States Congress passed the Defense of Marriage Act. It

Learn more about the **Supreme Court of the United States** at this site. Information on the Court's rules, opinions and orders, and biographies of the current justices are some of the areas covered on the Web site.

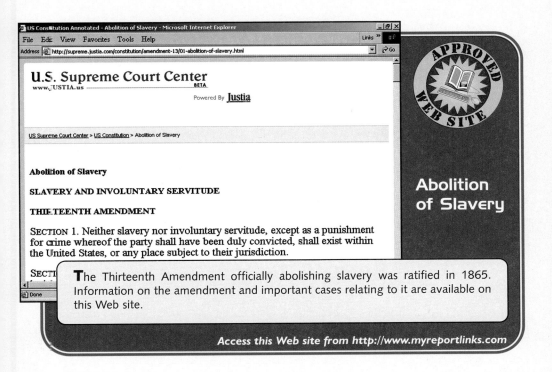

Access this Web site from http://www.myreportlinks.com

stated that the federal government would not recognize same-sex relationships as marriages for any purpose. It also stated that if a couple gets married in a state that recognizes same-sex marriage, another state does not have to recognize the relationship as a marriage if it chooses not to.

There is no doubt that the Supreme Court will continue to review and refine the parameters of the Thirteenth and Fourteenth Amendments as American society and American values change.

The Constitution of the United States

The text of the Constitution is presented here. All words are given their modern spelling and capitalization. Brackets [ ] indicate parts that have been changed or set aside by amendments.

Preamble

We the People of the United States, in Order to form a more perfect Union, establish Justice, insure domestic Tranquillity, provide for the common defence, promote the general Welfare, and secure the Blessings of Liberty to ourselves and our Posterity, do ordain and establish this Constitution for the United States of America.

Article I
The Legislative Branch

Section 1. All legislative powers herein granted shall be vested in a Congress of the United States, which shall consist of a Senate and House of Representatives.

The House of Representatives

Section 2. The House of Representatives shall be composed of members chosen every second year by the people of the several states, and the electors in each state shall have the qualifications requisite for electors of the most numerous branch of the state legislature.

No person shall be a Representative who shall not have attained to the age of twenty five years, and been seven years a citizen of the United States, and who shall not, when elected, be an inhabitant of that state in which he shall be chosen.

Representatives and direct taxes shall be apportioned among the several states which may be included within this union, according to their respective numbers, [which shall be determined by adding to the whole number of free persons, including those bound to service for a term of years, and excluding Indians not taxed, three fifths of all other persons]. The actual Enumeration shall be made within three years after the first meeting of the Congress of the United States, and within every subsequent term of ten years, in such manner as they shall by law direct. The number of Representatives shall not exceed one for every thirty thousand, but each state shall have at least one Representative; [and until such enumeration shall be made, the state of New Hampshire shall be entitled to chuse three, Massachusetts eight, Rhode Island and Providence Plantations one, Connecticut five, New York six, New Jersey four, Pennsylvania eight, Delaware one, Maryland six, Virginia ten, North Carolina five, South Carolina five, and Georgia three].

When vacancies happen in the Representation from any state, the executive authority thereof shall issue writs of election to fill such vacancies.

The House of Representatives shall choose their speaker and other officers; and shall have the sole power of impeachment.

The Senate

Section 3. The Senate of the United States shall be composed of two Senators from each state [chosen by the legislature thereof,] for six years; and each Senator shall have one vote.

Immediately after they shall be assembled in consequence of the first election, they shall be divided as equally as may be into three classes. The seats of the Senators of the first class shall be vacated at the expiration of the second year, of the second class at the expiration of the fourth year, and the third class at the expiration of the sixth year, so that one third may be chosen every second year; [and if vacancies happen by resignation, or otherwise, during the recess of the legislature of any state, the executive thereof may make temporary appointments until the next meeting of the legislature, which shall then fill such vacancies].

No person shall be a Senator who shall not have attained to the age of thirty years, and been nine years a citizen of the United States and who shall not, when elected, be an inhabitant of that state for which he shall be chosen.

The Vice President of the United States shall be President of the Senate, but shall have no vote, unless they be equally divided.

The Senate shall choose their other officers, and also a President pro tempore, in the absence of the Vice President, or when he shall exercise the office of President of the United States.

The Senate shall have the sole power to try all impeachments. When sitting for that purpose, they shall be on oath or affirmation. When the President of the United States is tried, the Chief Justice shall preside: And no person shall be convicted without the concurrence of two thirds of the members present.

Judgment in cases of impeachment shall not extend further than to removal from office, and disqualification to hold and enjoy any office of honor, trust or profit under the United States: but the party convicted shall nevertheless be liable and subject to indictment, trial, judgment and punishment, according to law.

Organization of Congress

Section 4. The times, places and manner of holding elections for Senators and Representatives, shall be prescribed in each state by the legislature thereof; but the Congress may at any time by law make or alter such regulations, [except as to the places of choosing senators].

The Congress shall assemble at least once in every year, [and such meeting shall be on the first Monday in December], unless they shall by law appoint a different day.

Section 5. Each House shall be the judge of the elections, returns and qualifications of its own members, and a majority of each shall constitute a quorum to do business; but a smaller number may adjourn from day to day, and may be authorized to compel the attendance of absent members, in such manner, and under such penalties as each House may provide.

Each House may determine the rules of its proceedings, punish its members for disorderly behavior, and, with the concurrence of two thirds, expel a member.

Each House shall keep a journal of its proceedings, and from time to time publish the same, excepting such parts as may in their judgment require secrecy; and the yeas and nays of the members of either House on any question shall, at the desire of one fifth of those present, be entered on the journal.

Neither House, during the session of Congress, shall, without the consent of the other, adjourn for more than three days, nor to any other place than that in which the two Houses shall be sitting.

Section 6. The Senators and Representatives shall receive a compensation for their services, to be ascertained by law, and paid out of the treasury of the United States. They shall in all cases, except treason, felony and breach of the peace, be privileged from arrest during their attendance at the session of their respective Houses, and in going to and returning from the same; and for any speech or debate in either House, they shall not be questioned in any other place.

No Senator or Representative shall, during the time for which he was elected, be appointed to any civil office under the authority of the United States, which shall have been created, or the emoluments whereof shall have been increased during such time: and no person holding any office under the United States, shall be a member of either House during his continuance in office.

Section 7. All bills for raising revenue shall originate in the House of Representatives; but the Senate may propose or concur with amendments as on other Bills.

Every bill which shall have passed the House of Representatives and the Senate, shall, before it become a law, be presented to the President of the United States; if he approve he shall sign it, but if not he shall return it, with his objections to that House in which it shall have originated, who shall enter the objections at large on their journal, and proceed to reconsider it. If after such reconsideration two thirds of that House shall agree to pass the bill, it shall be sent, together with the objections, to the other House, by which it shall likewise be reconsidered, and if approved by two thirds of that House, it shall become a law. But in all such cases the votes of both Houses shall be determined by yeas and nays, and the names of the persons voting for and against the bill shall be entered on the journal of each House respectively. If any bill shall not be returned by the President within ten days (Sundays excepted) after it shall have been presented to him, the same shall be a law, in like manner as if he had signed it, unless the Congress by their adjournment prevent its return, in which case it shall not be a law.

Every order, resolution, or vote to which the concurrence of the Senate and House of Representatives may be necessary (except on a question of adjournment) shall be presented to the President of the United States; and before the same shall take effect, shall be approved by him, or being disapproved by him, shall be repassed by two thirds of the Senate and House of Representatives, according to the rules and limitations prescribed in the case of a bill.

Powers Granted to Congress
The Congress shall have the power:

Section 8. To lay and collect taxes, duties, imposts and excises, to pay the debts and provide for the common defense and general welfare of the United States; but all duties, imposts and excises shall be uniform throughout the United States;

To borrow money on the credit of the United States;

To regulate commerce with foreign nations, and among the several states, and with the Indian tribes;

To establish a uniform rule of naturalization, and uniform laws on the subject of bankruptcies throughout the United States;

To coin money, regulate the value thereof, and of foreign coin, and fix the standard of weights and measures;

To provide for the punishment of counterfeiting the securities and current coin of the United States;

To establish post offices and post roads;

To promote the progress of science and useful arts, by securing for limited times to authors and inventors the exclusive right to their respective writings and discoveries;

To constitute tribunals inferior to the Supreme Court;

To define and punish piracies and felonies committed on the high seas, and offenses against the law of nations;

To declare war, grant letters of marque and reprisal, and make rules concerning captures on land and water;

To raise and support armies, but no appropriation of money to that use shall be for a longer term than two years;

To provide and maintain a navy;

To make rules for the government and regulation of the land and naval forces;

To provide for calling forth the militia to execute the laws of the union, suppress insurrections and repel invasions;

To provide for organizing, arming, and disciplining, the militia, and for governing such part of them as may be employed in the service of the United States, reserving to the states respectively, the appointment of the officers, and the authority of training the militia according to the discipline prescribed by Congress;

To exercise exclusive legislation in all cases whatsoever, over such District (not exceeding ten miles square) as may, by cession of particular states, and the acceptance of Congress, become the seat of the government of the United States, and to exercise like authority over all places purchased by the con ent of the legislature of the state in which the same shall be, for the erection of forts, magazines, arsenals, dockyards, and other needful buildings;—And

To make all laws which shall be necessary and proper for carrying into execution the foregoing powers, and all other powers vested by this Constitution in the government of the United States, or in any department or officer thereof.

Powers Forbidden to Congress

Section 9. The migration or importation of such persons as any of the states now existing shall think proper to admit, shall not be prohibited by the Congress prior to the year one thousand eight hundred and eight, but a tax or duty may be imposed on such importation, not exceeding ten dollars for each person.

The privilege of the writ of habeas corpus shall not be suspended, unless when in cases of rebellion or invasion the public safety may require it.

No bill of attainder or ex post facto law shall be passed.

No capitation, [or other direct,] tax shall be laid, unless in proportion to the census or enumeration herein before directed to be taken.

No tax or duty shall be laid on articles exported from any state.

No preference shall be given by any regulation of commerce or revenue to the ports of one state over those of another: nor shall vessels bound to, or from, one state, be obliged to enter, clear or pay duties in another.

No money shall be drawn from the treasury, but in consequence of appropriations made by law; and a regular statement and account of receipts and expenditures of all public money shall be published from time to time.

No title of nobility shall be granted by the United States: and no person holding any office of profit or trust under them, shall, without the consent of the Congress, accept of any present, emolument, office, or title, of any kind whatever, from any king, prince, or foreign state.

Powers Forbidden to the States

Section 10 No state shall enter into any treaty, alliance, or confederation; grant letters of marque and reprisal; coin money; emit bills of credit; make anything but gold and silver coin a tender in payment of debts; pass any bill of attainder, ex post facto law, or law impairing the obligation of contracts, or grant any title of nobility.

No state shall, without the consent of the Congress, lay any imposts or duties on imports or exports, except what may be absolutely necessary for executing its inspection laws: and the net produce of all duties and imposts, laid by any state on imports or exports, shall be for the use of the treasury of the United States; and all such laws shall be subject to the revision and control of the Congress.

No state shall, without the consent of Congress, lay any duty of tonnage, keep troops, or ships of war in time of peace, enter into any agreement or compact with another state, or with a foreign power, or engage in war, unless actually invaded, or in such imminent danger as will not admit of delay.

Article II
The Executive Branch

Section 1. The executive power shall be vested in a President of the United States of America. He shall hold his office during the term of four years, and, together with the Vice President, chosen for the same term, be elected, as follows:

Each state shall appoint, in such manner as the legislature thereof may direct, a number of electors, equal to the whole number of Senators and Representatives to which the State may be entitled in the Congress: but no Senator or Representative, or person holding an office of trust or profit under the United States, shall be appointed an elector.

[The electors shall meet in their respective states, and vote by ballot for two persons, of whom on at least shall not be an inhabitant of the same state with themselves. And they shall make a list c all the persons voted for, and of the number of votes for each; which list they shall sign and certify and transmit sealed to the seat of the government of the United States, directed to the President c the Senate. The President of the Senate shall, in the presence of the Senate and House of Represer tatives, open all the certificates, and the votes shall then be counted. The person having the greates number of votes shall be the President, if such number be a majority of the whole number of elec tors appointed; and if there be more than one who have such majority, and have an equal numbe of votes, then the House of Representatives shall immediately choose by ballot one of them for Pres ident; and if no person have a majority, then from the five highest on the list the said House shal in like manner choose the President. But in choosing the President, the votes shall be taken by States the representation from each state having one vote; A quorum for this purpose shall consist of member or members from two thirds of the states, and a majority of all the states shall be necessar to a choice. In every case, after the choice of the President, the person having the greatest number c votes of the electors shall be the Vice President. But if there should remain two or more who hav equal votes, the Senate shall choose from them by ballot the Vice President.]

The Congress may determine the time of choosing the electors, and the day on which they shall giv their votes; which day shall be the same throughout the United States.

No person except a natural born citizen, or a citizen of the United States, at the time of the adop tion of this Constitution, shall be eligible to the office of President; neither shall any person be eligible to that office who shall not have attained to the age of thirty-five years, and been fourteen Years a resident within the United States.

In case of the removal of the President from office, or of his death, resignation, or inability to dis charge the powers and duties of the said office, the same shall devolve on the Vice President, and the Congress may by law provide for the case of removal, death, resignation or inability, both of the Pres ident and Vice President, declaring what officer shall then act as President, and such officer shall ac accordingly, until the disability be removed, or a President shall be elected.

The President shall, at stated times, receive for his services, a compensation, which shall neither be increased nor diminished during the period for which he shall have been elected, and he shall no receive within that period any other emolument from the United States, or any of them.

Before he enter on the execution of his office, he shall take the following oath or affirmation:—"I do solemnly swear (or affirm) that I will faithfully execute the office of President of the United States and will to the best of my ability, preserve, protect and defend the Constitution of the United States.

Section 2. The President shall be commander-in-chief of the Army and Navy of the United States, and of the militia of the several states, when called into the actual service of the United States; he may require the opinion, in writing, of the principal officer in each of the executive departments, upor any subject relating to the duties of their respective offices, and he shall have power to grant reprieve and pardons for offenses against the United States, except in cases of impeachment.

He shall have power, by and with the advice and consent of the Senate, to make treaties, provided two-thirds of the Senators present concur; and he shall nominate, and by and with the advice and consent of the Senate, shall appoint ambassadors, other public ministers and consuls, judges of the Supreme Court, and all other officers of the United States, whose appointments are not herein otherwise provided for, and which shall be established by law: but the Congress may by law vest the appoint ment of such inferior officers, as they think proper, in the President alone, in the courts of law, or ir the heads of departments.

The President shall have power to fill up all vacancies that may happen during the recess of the Sen ate, by granting commissions which shall expire at the end of their next session.

Section 3. He shall from time to time give to the Congress information of the state of the union, and recommend to their consideration such measures as he shall judge necessary and expedient; he may n extraordinary occasions, convene both Houses, or either of them, and in case of disagreement etween them, with respect to the time of adjournment, he may adjourn them to such time as he hall think proper; he shall receive ambassadors and other public ministers; he shall take care that he laws be faithfully executed, and shall commission all the officers of the United States.

ection 4. The President, Vice President and all civil officers of the United States, shall be removed from ffice on impeachment for, and conviction of, treason, bribery, or other high crimes and misdemeanors.

Article III
The Judicial Branch

ection 1. The judicial power of the United States, shall be vested in one Supreme Court, and in such nferior courts as the Congress may from time to time ordain and establish. The judges, both of the upreme and inferior courts, shall hold their offices during good behaviour, and shall, at stated imes, receive for their services, a compensation, which shall not be diminished during their contin-ance in office.

ection 2. The judicial power shall extend to all cases, in law and equity, arising under this Constitu-ion, the laws of the United States, and treaties made, or which shall be made, under their uthority;—to all cases affecting ambassadors, other public ministers and consuls;—to all cases of dmiralty and maritime jurisdiction, [—to controversies to which the United States shall be a arty;—to controversies between two or more states, [between a state and citizens of another state;], etween citizens of different states;—between citizens of the same state, claiming lands under grants f different states, and between a state, or the citizens thereof, and foreign states, [citizens or subjects].

n all cases affecting ambassadors, other public ministers and consuls, and those in which a state hall be party, the Supreme Court shall have original jurisdiction. In all the other cases before men-ioned, the Supreme Court shall have appellate jurisdiction, both as to law and fact, with such xceptions, and under such regulations as the Congress shall make.

The trial of all crimes, except in cases of impeachment, shall be by jury; and such trial shall be held n the state where the said crimes shall have been committed; but when not committed within any tate, the trial shall be at such place or places as the Congress may by law have directed.

Section 3. Treason against the United States, shall consist only in levying war against them, or in adher-ng to their enemies, giving them aid and comfort. No person shall be convicted of treason unless on the testimony of two witnesses to the same overt act, or on confession in open court.

The Congress shall have power to declare the punishment of treason, but no attainder of treason shall work corruption of blood, or forfeiture except during the life of the person attainted.

Article IV
Relation of the States to Each Other

Section 1. Full faith and credit shall be given in each state to the public acts, records, and judicial pro-ceedings of every other state. And the Congress may by general laws prescribe the manner in which such acts records, and proceedings shall be proved, and the effect thereof.

Section 2. The citizens of each state shall be entitled to all privileges and immunities of citizens in the several states.

A person charged in any state with treason, felony, or other crime, who shall flee from justice, and be found in another state, shall on demand of the executive authority of the state from which he fled, be delivered up, to be removed to the state having jurisdiction of the crime.

[No person held to service or labor in one state, under the laws thereof, escaping into another, shall, in consequence of any law or regulation therein, be discharged from such service or labor, but shall be delivered up on claim of the party to whom such service or labor may be due.]

Federal-State Relations

Section 3. New states may be admitted by the Congress into this Union; but no new states shall be formed or erected within the jurisdiction of any other state, nor any state be formed by the junction of two or more states, without the consent of the legislatures of the states concerned, as well as of the Congress.

The Congress shall have power to dispose of and make all needful rules and regulations respecting the territory or other property belonging to the United States; and nothing in this Constitution shall be so construed as to prejudice any claims of the United States, or of any particular state.

Section 4. The United States shall guarantee to every state in this union a republican form of government, and shall protect each of them against invasion; and on application of the legislature, or of the executive (when the legislature cannot be convened) against domestic violence.

Article V
Amending the Constitution

The Congress, whenever two thirds of both houses shall deem it necessary, shall propose amendments to this Constitution, or, on the application of the legislatures of two thirds of the several states, shall call a convention for proposing amendments, which, in either case, shall be valid to all intents and purposes, as part of this Constitution, when ratified by the legislatures of three fourths of the several states, or by conventions in three fourths thereof, as the one or the other mode of ratification may be proposed by the Congress; provided [that no amendment which may be made prior to the year one thousand eight hundred and eight shall in any manner affect the first and fourth clauses in the ninth section of the first article; and] that no state, without its consent, shall be deprived of its equal suffrage in the Senate.

Article VI
National Debts

All debts contracted and engagements entered into, before the adoption of this Constitution, shall be as valid against the United States under this Constitution, as under the Confederation.

Supremacy of the National Government

This Constitution, and the laws of the United States which shall be made in pursuance thereof; and all treaties made, or which shall be made, under the authority of the United States, shall be the supreme law of the land; and the judges in every state shall be bound thereby, anything in the constitution or laws of any State to the contrary notwithstanding.

The senators and representatives before mentioned, and the members of the several state legislatures, and all executive and judicial officers, both of the United States and of the several states, shall be bound by oath or affirmation, to support this Constitution; but no religious test shall ever be required as a qualification to any office or public trust under the United States.

Article VII
Ratifying the Constitution

The ratification of the conventions of nine states, shall be sufficient for the establishment of this Constitution between the states so ratifying the same.

Done in convention by the unanimous consent of the states present the seventeenth day of September in the year of our Lord one thousand seven hundred and eighty seven and of the independence of the United States of America the twelfth. In witness whereof we have hereunto subscribed our Names.

Thirteenth Amendment

Section 1. Neither slavery nor involuntary servitude, except as a punishment for crime where of the party shall have been duly convicted, shall exist within the United States, or any place subject to their jurisdiction.

Section 2. Congress shall have the power to enforce this article by appropriate legislation.

Fourteenth Amendment

Section 1. All persons born or naturalized in the United States, and subject to the jurisdiction thereof, are citizens of the United States and of the State wherein they reside. No State shall make or enforce any law which shall abridge the privileges or immunities of citizens of the United States; nor shall any State deprive any person of life, liberty, or property, without due process of law; nor deny to any person within its jurisdiction the equal protection of the laws.

Section 2. Representatives shall be apportioned among the several States according to their respective numbers, counting the whole number of persons in each State, excluding Indians not taxed. But when the right to vote at any election for the choice of electors for President and Vice President of the United States, Representatives in Congress, the Executive and Judicial officers of a State, or the members of the Legislature thereof, is denied to any of the male inhabitants of such State, being twenty-one years of age, and citizens of the United States, or in any way abridged, except for participation in rebellion, or other crime, the basis of representation therein shall be reduced in the proportion which the number of such male citizens shall bear to the whole number of male citizens twenty-one years of age in such State.

Section 3. No one shall be a Senator or Representative in Congress, or elector of President and Vice President, or hold any office, civil or military, under the United States, or under any State, who, having previously taken an oath, as a member of Congress, or as an officer of the United States, or as a member of any State legislature, or as an executive or judicial officer of any State, to support the Constitution of the United States, shall have engaged in insurrection or rebellion against the same, or given aid or comfort to the enemies thereof. But Congress may by a vote of two-thirds of each House, remove such disability.

Section 4. The validity of the public debt of the United States, authorized by law, including debts incurred for payment of pensions and bounties or services in suppressing insurrection or rebellion, shall not be questioned. But neither the United States nor any State shall assume or pay any debt or obligation incurred in aid of insurrection or rebellion against the United States, or any claim for the loss or emancipation of any slave; but all such debts, obligations and claims shall be held illegal and void.

Section 5. The Congress shall have power to enforce, by appropriate legislation, the provisions of this article.

Report Links

**The Internet sites described below can be accessed at
http://www.myreportlinks.com**

▶**The Charters of Freedom: The Constitution**
Editor's Choice Read the U.S. Constitution on the National Archives Web site.

▶**The African American Odyssey: A Quest for Full Citizenship**
Editor's Choice This Library of Congress exhibit showcases America's quest for equality.

▶**"I Will Be Heard"—Abolitionism in America**
Editor's Choice This is a Cornell University Libraries online exhibit on the abolition movement in America.

▶**The Thirteenth Amendment: The Abolition of Slavery**
Editor's Choice Study the Constitutional history of slavery on this site.

▶**U.S. Constitution: Fourteenth Amendment**
Editor's Choice Text of the Fourteenth Amendment is available on this site.

▶**The African American: A Journey From Slavery to Freedom**
Editor's Choice This site is devoted to understanding the legacy of slavery.

▶**Abolition, Anti-Slavery Movements, and the Rise of the Sectional Controversy**
The Library of Congress examines slavery on this Web page.

▶**Abolition of Slavery**
You can read analysis and interpretation of the Thirteenth Amendment at this site.

▶**Abraham Lincoln**
This is a biography of the sixteenth president.

▶**Africans in America**
A comprehensive overview of slavery.

▶**American Civil War**
This extensive Web site is a clearinghouse for information on the Civil War.

▶**The American Civil War: Forging a More Perfect Union**
The National Park Service's has posted this Web site on the American Civil War.

▶**The Articles of Confederation**
Yale Law School has the text of the Articles on this Web site.

▶**The Black Past**
For reference materials on African American history, visit this site.

▶**The Civil Rights Case**
On this site you can read Frederick Douglas's speech in reaction to the 1883 *Civil Rights Cases* court decision.

Report Links

The Internet sites described below can be accessed at http://www.myreportlinks.com

▶ **The Civil Rights Cases, (1883)**
This site provides a good overview of the five cases.

▶ **Documenting the American South**
This electronic collection of resources examines the culture and history of the American South.

▶ **The *Dred Scott* Case**
Primary documents for the *Dred Scott* case can be viewed on this site.

▶ **Fourteenth Amendment**
Read the text of the Fourteenth Amendment.

▶ **Human Smuggling/Trafficking: The Trade in People**
This article discusses human smuggling and what the Canadian government is doing about it.

▶ **In the Courts**
This is good overview of the court cases that led up to *Brown* v. *Board of Education*.

▶ ***Plessy* v. *Ferguson*: Justice Harlan Dissents**
This is an excerpt from Justice Harlan's dissent of the decision.

▶ **Slavery and the Making of America**
This PBS site provides a look at the history of African slaves in America.

▶ **Supreme Court of the United States**
The official site of the Supreme Court of the United States.

▶ **The Supreme Court: The First Hundred Years**
At this site, you can read about the Supreme Court and its history.

▶ **Understanding the Federal Courts**
Learn more about the federal court system in the United States from this Web site.

▶ **The United States' Effort to Combat Trafficking in Persons**
This journal article explains what the government is doing about modern-day slavery.

▶ ***United States* v. *Kozminski*, (1988)**
Read an overview of this Thirteenth Amendment court decision, on this site.

▶ **Victims of Trafficking and Violence Protection Act of 2000**
This recent government report provides a comprehensive guide to modern slavery.

▶ ***Yick Wo* v. *Hopkins*, (1886)**
Learn more about this important court decision on this FindLaw Web site.

abolition—The movement and legal ending of slavery of African Americans in the United States.

case law—Law established by previous legal decisions.

claimant—A person who makes an assertion in court.

Confederacy—Abbreviated name for the Confederate States of America, the states that had seceded from the United States of America and fought against the Union during the Civil War. It was made up of South Carolina, Mississippi, Florida, Alabama, Georgia, Louisiana, Texas, Virginia, Arkansas, Tennessee, and North Carolina.

copperhead—A person who lived in the North but supported the South during the Civil War and Reconstruction.

discrimination—Treatment or consideration based on class or category rather than on merit.

disenfranchise—To remove or deprive a person of their rights of citizenship or the right to vote.

disparity—Large difference.

emancipation—Freeing an individual from the control of another individual or group.

forced labor—Employment against one's will often under threat of violence or coercion.

fugitive slave—A slave who has escaped from his or her master.

indentured servant—A person who is bound to work for another in order to repay expenses.

institution—A significant organization or system in a society.

jurisdiction—The power, right, or authority to interpret and apply the law.

naturalized citizen—A person who was not born in the United States but became a citizen after emigrating from another country.

peonage—A system by which debtors are bound to their creditors until their debts are paid.

precedent—Something done or said that may serve as an example to authorize or justify an act of the same or a similar kind.

ratify—To approve a law or amendment, making it active.

secede—To separate from an organization.

segregate—To separate or set apart from others or from the general mass.

slavery—The state of being bound in service as property of an individual or group.

statute—A law enacted by the legislative branch of a government.

trafficking—Trade in a specific commodity or service, often illegal, such as drug trafficking or human trafficking.

Chapter 1. Life During Wartime

1. Bruce Catton, *American Heritage History of the Civil War* (New York: Random House, 1998), pp. 230–241.

2. Akhil Reed Amar, *America's Constitution, A Biography* (New York: Random House, 2006), pp. 354, 356, 358.

3. Ibid.

4. Richard D. Heffner, *A Documentary History of the United States* (New York: Signet Books, 2002), pp. 183–185.

Chapter 2. The History of Slavery

1. Richard Middleton, *Colonial America: A History, 1607–1760* (Cambridge, Mass.: Blackwell Publishers 1992) pp. 40–41.

2. WPA Writer's Program, *Virginia: Guide to the Old Dominion* (New York: Oxford University Press, 1940), p. 378.

3. Jack N. Rakove, *Founding America, Documents from the Revolution to the Bill of Rights* (New York: Barnes & Noble Classics, 2006) pp. 126–127.

4. Benjamin Quarles, *The Negro in the American Revolution* (New York: W. W. Norton and Company, 1973), p. 119.

5. Alexander Hamilton, James Madison and John Jay, *The Federalist Papers* (New York: Bantam Classics, 2003), pp. ix-xiii.

6. Catherine Drinker Bowen, *Miracle at Philadelphia* (New York: Little Brown and Company, 1986), pp. 197–204.

7. Akhil Reed Amar, *America's Constitution, A Biography* (New York: Random House, 2006), p. 119.

8. Douglas Brinkley, *American Heritage History of the United States* (New York: Viking, 1998), pp. 184–185.

9. Bruce Catton, *American Heritage History of the Civil War* (New York: Random House, 1998), p. 32.

10. Norman Redlich, John Attanasio, and Joel K. Goldstein, *Understanding Constitutional Law* (Newark, N.J.: Matthew Bender & Company, 2005) pp. 362–363.

11. Bruce Catton, *American Heritage History of the Civil War* (New York: Random House, 1998), pp. 230–241.

Chapter 3. The New Amendments

1. Theodore J. Lowi and Benjamin Ginsberg, *American Government: Freedom and Power, Second Edition* (New York: W. W. Norton & Company, 1992), p. 114.

2. Bruce Catton, *American Heritage History of the Civil War* (New York: Random House, 1998), pp. 230–241.

Chapter 4. The Amendments and the Legal System

1. *Strauder* v. *West Virginia,* 100 U.S. 303 (1880).

2. Civil Rights Cases, 109 U.S. 3 (1883).

3. *Yick Wo* v. *Hopkins,* 118 U.S. 356 (1886).

4. *Plessy* v. *Ferguson,* 163 U.S. 537 (1896).

5. *Plessy* v. *Ferguson,* 163 U.S. 537 (1896).

6. *United States* v. *Wong Kim Ark,* 169 U.S. 649 (1989).

7. *Gitlow* v. *New York,* 268 U.S. 652 (1925).

8. Norman Redlich, John Attanasio, and Joel K. Goldstein *Understanding Constitutional Law* (Newark, N.J.: Matthew Bender & Company, 2005) pp. 501–502.

9. *Lum* v. *Rice,* 275 U.S. 78 (1927).

10. *Missouri ex rel. Gaines* v. *Canada,* 305 U.S. 337 (1938).

11. *Smith* v. *Allwright,* 321 U.S. 649 (1944).

12. *Sweatt* v. *Painter,* 339 U.S. 629 (1950).

13. *Brown* v. *Board of Education,* 347 U.S. 483 (1954).

14. Ibid.

15. *Gideon* v. *Wainwright,* 372 U.S. 335 (1963).

16. *Loving* v. *Virginia,* 388 U.S. 1 (1967).

17. *Goldberg* v. *Kelly,* 397 U.S. 254 (1970).

18. *Mississippi University for Women* v. *Hogan,* 458 U.S. 718 (1982).

Chapter 5. Modern Slavery

1. *United States* v. *Kozminski,* 487 U.S. 931 (1988).

2. *United States* v. *Virginia,* 518 U.S. 515 (1996).

Greene, Meg. *Into the Land of Freedom: African Americans in Reconstruction.* Minneapolis: Lerner Publications, Co., 2004.

Hudson, Jr., David L. *The Fourteenth Amendment: Equal Protection under the Law.* Berkeley Heights, N.J.: Enslow Publishers, 2002.

Martin, Michael J. *Emancipation Proclamation: Hope of Freedom for the Slaves.* Mankato, Minn.: Bridgestone Books, 2003.

McKissack, Patricia C. and Fredrick L. *Days of Jubilee: The End of Slavery in the United States.* New York: Scholastic Press, 2003.

McNeese, Tim. *The Abolitionist Movement: Ending Slavery.* New York: Chelsea House, 2007.

Nardo, Don. *The U.S. Constitution.* San Diego, Calif.: Kidhaven Press, 2002.

Rossi, Ann M. *Freedom Struggle: The Anti-Slavery Movement, 1830—1865.* Washington, D.C.: National Geographic, 2005.

Ruggiero, Adriane. *Reconstruction.* New York: Marshall Cavendish Benchmark, 2007.

Stefoff, Rebecca. *The Civil War and Reconstruction: 1863—1877.* New York: Benchmark Books, 2003.

Weidner, Daniel. *The Constitution: The Preamble and the Articles.* Berkeley Heights, N.J.: Enslow Publishers, 2002.

Theme

3. It was Rebecca's turn to cook dinner. Rebecca did not like to cook. So on her night, she usually heated up a few cans of chili, or cooked a frozen pizza. "This pizza is no good," her brother Frank said. "It tastes like cardboard. The cheese tastes like rubber." Rebecca thought that Frank's complaint was petty, especially since he ate everything on his plate. "I am going to make a pizza every time it is my turn to cook," Rebecca said. "Since I know that you will eat it."

a) duplicity   b) fairness   c) effort

4. Wendy enjoyed spending time with her grandmother. Her grandmother told her stories about what the world was like when she was a little girl, a very long time ago. Wendy also liked her grandmother's caramel cake and blackberry cobbler. There was only one problem. Wendy's grandmother always made casseroles for dinner. Wendy didn't want to hurt her grandmother's feelings. But she hated casseroles, and she couldn't help hesitating before taking a bite. But she did take a bite, because she loved the way that her grandmother's eyes lit up when she saw Wendy eating her home-cooked food. When Wendy's grandmother smiled, suddenly the casserole didn't taste so bad.

Theme

FROM KEY WORD TO THEME

A good first step towards understanding **theme** is to identify a key word or concept that a story deals with. For example, a story might be about courage, friendship, or bravery. But a **theme** cannot be expressed in a single word. The subject or key word of a story might be friendship, but the **theme** is something particular about friendship that can be expressed in a complete sentence.

Read the passages below. For each one, circle the key word that best describes what the passage is about. Then, think about the passage and write a sentence that includes that key word, and which expresses its **theme**. Remember, **theme** is bigger than just the story itself; it is a lesson or a message that is applicable in the real world.

1. Kim's diet was terrible. All she ate was chips and sweets and jelly sandwiches on white bread.

because of what she was eating, Kim was amazed. She didn't realize that she had so much power to make herself feel better. Kim stopped eating junk food and started eating fruits and vegetables. In a few weeks she felt like a new person.

a) courage   b) responsibility   c) health

2. Dan was really looking forward to eating some cake. But when his mother sliced the cake, she made the pieces very small. "Why is my piece so small?" Dan asked, dismayed. "Because there are a lot of people here," his mother told him. "We have to make sure that we have enough cake for everybody. His mother continued to cut and serve the cake and soon there was no more cake left. Disappointed that he would not be able to have seconds, Dan went off to sit and eat his tiny piece of cake. There was a small girl sitting at his table. She looked longingly at Dan's cake. "I did not get any cake," she said. "By the time I got up there, all of the cake was gone." "Here," Dan said, handing the girl a fork. "I will share my cake with you." The little girl's face lit up, and suddenly Dan felt better.

a) hunger   b) generosity   c) disappointment

CCSS. RL.5.2 | © http://www.englishworksheetsland.com

5. Ryan's mother was trying to learn to cook. She was not very good at it, though. One night she burned the casserole. Another night she scalded the soup. Ryan and his father did their best to eat what she put in front of them, though. "She will get better," Ryan's father told Ryan. "We have to encourage her so that she will not give up." One afternoon Ryan's mother put too much baking soda in the cookies and they were so bitter that Ryan had to spit a bite of cookie out into his napkin when his mother wasn't looking. "I am sorry that I am not a good cook," his mother told him. "That is okay," Ryan said. "The important thing is that you keep working on it, and then you will get better."

a) perseverance   b) honesty   c) cooking

_____